SWOOPE ALMANAC

*Stories of love, land, and water
in Virginia's Shenandoah Valley*

Robert Whitescarver

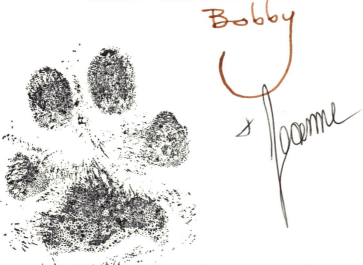

Copyright 2019 © Robert Whitescarver

All rights reserved. No part of this book may be reproduced, stored in a retrieval system, or transmitted, in any form or by any means, electronic, mechanical, photocopying, recording, or otherwise, without the written permission of the author.

Cover design and interior layout by Jennifer Wood.

For information about ordering books
or to contact the author,
visit www.SwoopeAlmanac.org

Library of Congress Control Number: 2018966451
ISBN: 9781934368459

Published by Lot's Wife Publishing
P.O. Box 1844
Staunton, VA 24402
www.LotsWifePublishing.com
email: lotswife@comcast.net

Printed by Mid Valley Press
Verona, Virginia

Dedicated to my parents
Margaret Garrett Whitescarver
Charles Kyle Whitescarver Jr.

CONTENTS

ILLUSTRATIONS vi
ENDORSEMENTS viii
FOREWORDS x
PREFACE xii
ACKNOWLEDGMENTS xiii
INTRODUCTION xvi

SECTION I   Swoope Almanac

  1   Life on the Farm 3
  2   Funny Stories, Wandering Thoughts,
        and Laments 35
  3   Winter 83
  4   Spring 95
  5   Summer 107
  6   Fall 119

SECTION II   My Life's Work

  7   Riparian Buffers 133
  8   Calls for Action 167
  9   Hope for Agriculture 205
 10   Bird Species in Steep Decline in Swoope . . . 231
 11   Invasive Species 243

EPILOGUE 259
ABOUT THE AUTHOR 261

ILLUSTRATIONS

Roni Freeman (Pages 2, 34, 44, 92, 106, 204, 242)

Betty Gatewood (Pages 1, 82, 94, 118, 130, 132, 230)

Neal Whitescarver (Page 166)

PHOTOS

Cover Photos, Bobby Whitescarver
Inside Back Cover, Charles K. Whitescarver III
Inside Front Cover, Bobby Whitescarver

ICONS

Journal Entries
(Roni Freeman)

Articles
(Betty Gatewood)

The publication of this book was made possible by grants from the Keith Campbell Foundation for the Environment and from George Ohrstrom II

ENDORSEMENTS

I have not met a more capable person than Bobby to explain, in understandable terms, the challenges we face in agriculture today and the opportunities before us to rise above them.

While so many people today carry a message of alarm and defeatism, Bobby carries a message of optimism and offers concrete solutions, many of which he and his wife, Jeanne, have implemented with their own hands on their own land.

This book is a must-read for anyone concerned about the Chesapeake Bay and how best to work constructively with farmers to chart a sustainable path forward.

Jeff Corbin
Former Senior Advisor to the EPA
Administrator for Chesapeake Bay

At its core, this book is an incredible love story: the love that Bobby has for Jeanne; the love they both have for their life on the farm, their land, their animals; their love of community; and the love they share for the environment—all told through a series of daily vignettes. Bobby has captured and transformed ordinary moments into extraordinary life lessons.

Nicholas DiPasquale
Former EPA Director,
Chesapeake Bay Program

There's often a story about cattle, a little talk of environmental concerns, and a mention of his "Princess" and her collaborative work with him. That's how conversations go when I get a chance to visit with Bobby. He's easygoing and always has a great story, but there's a wealth of shared experience, knowledge, and love of farming and our environment in everything Bobby does. This latest book is just like sitting down and visiting with Bobby. You'll enjoy every bit of it.

Emmett W. Hanger Jr.
Virginia Senator

If you want to understand the perspective of a dedicated cattle farmer, educated ecologist, and water-quality specialist, this is the book for you!

Turn these pages and feel the frost on your nose in winter, hear quail calling in the spring, taste a homegrown tomato in the summer, and watch Monarch butterflies fuel up on nectar in the fall... truly spectacular stuff!

George Ohrstrom II
Founder,
The Downstream Project

FOREWORDS

I want to be a farmer!

That's the impact Bobby's Swoope Almanac had on me. His journal entries bring his heartfelt experiences to life for his reader, stirring emotions from sorrow over a dead calf to laughter over some of the raucous events he and his wife and partner, Jeanne, experience on their farm. As he often mentions, he can't get over how fortunate he is to live in Swoope and to have found the love of his life.

You don't have to be a farmer or want to be a farmer to get the messages in the Swoope Almanac, but it helps to allow yourself to be enveloped in the atmosphere Bobby creates as he reflects on life on the farm and recounts the experiences that make up that life.

With his professional background, Bobby could have written this book as scientific treatise, but it is anything but. His thirty years of experience as a field officer with the Natural Resources Conservation Service and his interaction with farmers over conservation issues, such as keeping cows out of the streams that course through their Shenandoah Valley farms, brings a practical view to the needs of farmers. He is a passionate farmer himself and, without preaching, he makes the case for the environmental contributions that can be made at the farm level to benefit the health of all downstream life, while preserving and enhancing the financial return on the farm.

AND . . . it's a fun read.

D. Keith Campbell
Investment Advisor and Founder,
the Campbell Foundation
Baltimore, Maryland

This is a wonderful and earthy collection of essays that I find extremely refreshing. It's about wildlife and farm animals and the challenges associated with operating a productive farm in an environmentally sustainable way. I say earthy because Bobby is a naturalist first and foremost and exudes both an appreciation and reverence for nature in all his writings. He draws on over three decades of practical, hands-on experience with the USDA's Natural Resources Conservation Service working with landowners to design, implement, and install best management practices. But instead of preaching what he knows, he translates the multitude of highly technical environmental facts and figures in his head into easily absorbed sound bytes and delivers them in a "good old boy" style that is very effective. Despite a laid-back, down-country approach to delivering his essays, speeches, blogs, and op-ed pieces, his work is technically sound and taps into the current science surrounding each issue. This reflects both his deep intellectual capacity and his dedication to getting it right! And, knowing Bobby, you can thank him, not by sending him accolades, but rather by sharing notes of how you have made the environment of your backyard or workspace, whatever it may be, just a little bit better by heeding his advice and perspective on nature and weaving it into all the activities of your life. Enjoy the essays . . . enjoy Bobby . . . enjoy making that difference!

Bern Sweeney
Past President and Executive Director,
Stroud Water Research Center
Avondale, Pennsylvania

PREFACE

Jeanne Trimble Hoffman and I live on a working farm. We care about the cattle on that farm. We also care about the soil in the fields, the wildlife on the land, and the water that flows through the farm. I wrote this book to share the experiences of living on that working farm—a farm that produces great food and clean water. Farming for a living and adhering to good conservation practices can sometimes be at odds. That doesn't have to be the case. This book chronicles the story of how these two lifestyles were made to work in harmony.

It is a journey of love. Love of the land and water in the Shenandoah Valley of Virginia. And it is about the love that two people share on this wonderful journey.

This book is a continuation of my life's work of helping people appreciate the natural world around them and of making the world a better place for them and everyone downstream and into the future.

ACKNOWLEDGMENTS

I have so many people to thank for the production of this book. First, I must thank my wife and first line editor, Jeanne Trimble Hoffman, the main character in the book, my partner, and the love of my life. She is the reason the stories on these pages are so full of wonder. She never ceases to amaze me.

This book would not have been possible without the support of my friend Keith Campbell. We met at a Chesapeake Bay Foundation (CBF) function on the banks of the Potomac River in 2002, and he has encouraged me to continue fighting for clean water ever since. The mission of the Keith Campbell Foundation for the Environment is to improve water quality and ecological balance in the Bay and its rivers, as a healthy Bay fosters a vibrant regional economy and provides exceptional recreational opportunities. I am grateful for the Campbell Foundation's funding and support of my work and this book.

George L. Ohrstrom II also provided encouragement and support. A longtime fighter for clean water, George founded The Downstream Project—a conservation nonprofit that helps people like me and many organizations get their environmental messages out in front of the public.

Nancy Sorrells, of Lot's Wife Publishing, gave encouragement, support, editing, and publishing. Finding a publisher for the book was daunting at first, but she gave me the confidence I needed to push ahead. She is a very effective fighter for the environment because she does her research and backs her causes with science and logic—essential qualities for an editor and publisher.

Libby Howard provided excellent editing services. She has forgotten more than I will ever know about style and editing. She is a master at the intricacies of editing. Who would have thought when I started this project that I would be learning the difference between an "en" dash and an "em" dash?

Bill Howard and the Downstream Project provided leadership, website design, internet support, and marketing services. The Downstream Project stimulates awareness, action, and alliances through visual arts and technology. When I retired from the Natural Resources Conservation Service (NRCS) in 2011, Downstream helped me design my website and award-winning blog. Downstream also published my first e-book, *Bobby's Seven Principles of Selling Riparian Forest Buffers*.

Jennifer Wood, the book's graphic designer and my Swoope neighbor, brought her talent and flair to the project. She was able to meld the project team's ideas into a beautiful cover and interior design that helps take readers on a journey through the Shenandoah Valley.

The illustrators were so helpful and working with them was easy. Betty Gatewood has been drawing and journaling nature for years. She let me select the drawings for this book from hundreds of excellent choices. Roni Freeman, a former illustrator for the Smithsonian, eagerly took up the challenge to draw scenes of Swoope. My son, Neal, a lifelong artist, provided the illustration of me planting a tree.

The Chesapeake Bay Foundation has been a friend and supporter for decades. When I was still working for NRCS in the Valley, they sent Libby Norris to assist field offices with conservation efforts. She was great help, and when I retired in 2011 she encouraged the foundation to hire me as a private contractor. I have been working for the foundation ever since. Their mission is simple but strong—Save the Bay.

Conservation Services Inc., a tree planting company and distributor of tree shelters provided marketing support. When I asked its president, Lowry Tucker Jr., whether his company would plant a tree for every book sold, he said, "We are all about that!"

I would also like to thank Joe McCue and the Friends of Middle River. I remember well when Joe came into my office at NRCS and volunteered to plant trees. He knew then that we had a daunting mission and wanted to find out how he could help us get more conservation on the ground. He founded Conservation Services Inc., one of the largest tree planting companies on the East Coast, which became the North American distributor of Tubex tree shelters. He was also the first president of the Friends of Middle River, a nonprofit that not only raises awareness of the river but also helps farmers maintain riparian buffers.

Thanks also to all my coworkers in the Natural Resources Conservation Service, Farm Service Agency, Soil and Water Conservation Districts, and Virginia Department of Forestry for helping build a robust team of conservationists. You gave me a wonderful place to carry out a fulfilling career.

Many thanks to all the tree planters and all the farmers and landowners who have fenced their livestock out of streams and planted trees. Because of you we have cleaner streams and a healthier Chesapeake Bay. Farmers in the Bay watershed have already reduced by half their share of nutrients reaching the Bay.

And last, thanks to all the young people and students I've taught. They give me hope—hope that one day we will indeed reestablish Brook Trout in Middle River.

INTRODUCTION

Swoope is where I live. Although it has two *o*'s, it rhymes with hope. It's named after Jacob Swoope, a very prominent early settler to the southern end of the Shenandoah Valley in western Virginia. He was the first mayor of the city of Staunton.

Swoope is an absolutely gorgeous place. On top of the high hill behind our house, I can see forever. Looking north, the blue Allegheny Mountains extend as far as the eye can see on the left. Straight ahead are rolling green hills full of luscious green pastures and scattered barns with silos. Far to the right are the Blue Ridge Mountains that extend forever northward as well. On some days, an armada of big, white, puffy clouds moves east across the blue sky. Beneath my feet is the soil that has sustained and defined this Valley for millennia. Soil born from limestone, it is deep, mineral rich, and well drained.

There's a river. It flows north, collecting all the seeps, small streams, and runoff that flows from these hills. It's called the Middle River. Sixty-one river miles downstream from this spot, it helps form the South Fork of the Shenandoah River. Jed Hotchkiss, Civil War mapmaker for General Stonewall Jackson, wrote in 1885 that Middle River was "the chief river of the county, having the largest gathering ground and volume of any."

Two-hundred and fifty miles downstream, our water flows into the Potomac River at Harpers Ferry, West Virginia. A hundred miles from there, our water continues its flow into the nation's largest estuary—the Chesapeake Bay.

All the lands of Swoope lie within what hydrologists call the Upper Middle River watershed. The River is polluted and appears on the state's official Impaired Waters List because it exceeds the state standard for *E. coli* bacteria. The water also has too much sediment in it; it can't support a healthy aquatic ecosystem. And the water is not healthy for humans to wade in. Virginia's report on the pollution in the Upper Middle River watershed states that ninety-four percent of the *E. coli* pollution is from livestock.

I'm a soil and water conservationist. I've spent my entire adult life learning and teaching about building healthier soil and producing cleaner water. My career began after I graduated from Virginia Tech with a degree in soil science. In 1980 I began work as a soil conservationist in Fauquier County, Virginia, with the U.S. Department of Agriculture's Soil Conservation Service.

It was a fantastic job, and I feel so fortunate to have had a vocation that honored my college degree and my passion for sustainability. The job served me well as I gained so much knowledge and many life experiences from the people I worked with all over the Commonwealth of Virginia.

In 2000 I accepted a joint position with USDA and the Virginia Department of Conservation and Recreation that would fuel my desire for clean streams. I was the Virginia Technical Coordinator for the Conservation Reserve Enhancement Program (CREP) and was on loan from USDA to help design the program and train field staff in its implementation. But I didn't want to go to field offices across the state to just train personnel in procedures. My deal was this: if you want me to come to your office and train your staff, I will, but we must lay out a job on a farm with enrollment intentions. It was hands-on work; we drove stakes in the ground to delineate fence lines excluding livestock from hundreds of miles of streams. My plan and CREP worked. Hundreds of farmers signed up for the program in its first year.

In 2002 I returned to my former job as the district conservationist in the Headwaters Soil and Water Conservation District, which serves Augusta County, Virginia, and the cities of Staunton and Waynesboro. CREP was going strong. We had a great team to implement the program. Each year more and more farmers enrolled, and in 2010 we finally met our goal of forty miles of stream banks excluded from livestock in a single year, in a single conservation district. That was the best conservation team I ever worked with: John Kaylor, Cathy Perry, Bobby Drumheller, Hunter Musser, Jake Leonard, Patti Nylander, Lee Womack, Mark Hollberg, and all the folks at Conservation Services LLC, including Jeff Brower, David Coleman, and Joe McCue, its founder.

In 2011 I retired from federal service and started an environmental consulting business: Whitescarver Natural Resources Management LLC. The Chesapeake Bay Foundation hired me as a private consultant, and I have worked for it and other environmental organizations ever since. The Downstream Project, founded by George Ohrstrom, created and manages my website, gettingmoreontheground.com.

More than fifteen years ago, through luck, good fortune, or "divine order," as my late, dear mother would have said, I met Jeanne Trimble Hoffman. I was single and living alone in the tenant house of Grey Gables Farm in Swoope. The landlord, Victoria Godfrey, introduced us. Jeanne was a rural route mail carrier in Swoope.

I gave Jeanne a can of spray paint to mark where I should put my mailbox along the road. The next day I found a note on my door: "You are now a marked man."

A couple of years later, I married her, the love of my dreams, a ninth-generation farmer. She's the only ninth-generation farmer I've met. She's a hard-working farmer who wears pearl earrings every day, well deserving the title I gave her: Princess of Swoope. Turn the pages, and you will see why I have bestowed royalty status upon her.

Opposites really do attract. She loves cows; I love clean water. She wants more grass; I want more riparian buffers. When we drive through the pastures checking cattle, she constantly makes lists of things we need to do, like rehang a gate, fix fences, or cut down thistles. I, on the other hand, am observing all the wonderful natural happenings, like the song of an Eastern Meadowlark or the first Bobolink to arrive.

Jeanne and her mother, Jean Trimble Hoffman, raise beef cattle on the same farm their ancestor John Trimble acquired in 1746. Jeanne and her mother both love the land and the cattle.

Jeanne and Jean would never tell anyone how many acres of land they have. Asking a farmer how much land she has is like asking her how much money she has in her bank account. Whenever someone asks Jeanne how many acres she farms, she replies, "When the cows are grazing there is not enough pasture, and when I'm bush hogging, there is too much."

Jean and Jeanne's operation, Hoffman Farms, is a collection of several farms. But one of the farms is Jeanne's—the one that Middle River flows through.

This is the farm that taught soil and water man Bobby and cow woman Jeanne how to respect each other, love each other, compromise, and see and feel and touch and smell the results, which are far greater than each other's individual deeds and needs.

In 1949 *A Sand County Almanac* was published. The book is about Aldo Leopold's journey to restore the farmland and waters on his farm with sandy soil in Wisconsin. His book is a collection of essays about the land, water, and wildlife on that farm.

My book, *Swoope Almanac*, is modeled after his style of writing. It's a collection of essays, blog posts, poems, published articles, and journal entries about my journey with the Princess of Swoope, improving the resources on this farm in Swoope and creating the many stories of our life together—the joys, sorrows, triumphs, and defeats. They are stories of love, land, and water in Virginia's Shenandoah Valley.

Robert "Bobby" Whitescarver
Earth Day 2019

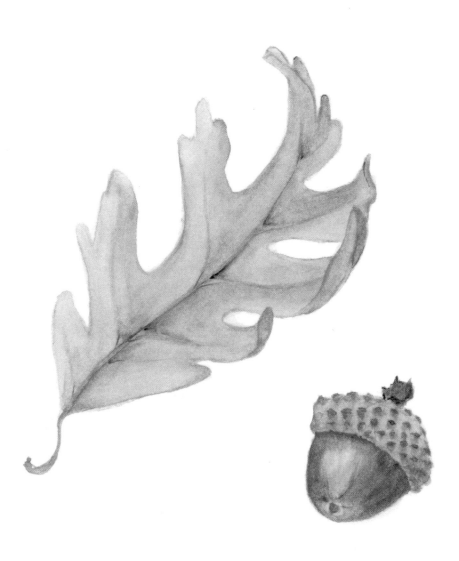

SECTION I

SWOOPE ALMANAC

This is a collection of journal entries, essays, and blog posts written about life on the farm and natural events occurring in Swoope, Virginia, our home, in America's legendary Shenandoah Valley. They were written from 2003 to 2018.

1
Life on the Farm

Jeanne Ropes a Calf from the Back of the Pickup Truck

I was riding shotgun in the pickup truck as we went to tag newborn calves. My job was to catch the newborn calf, put him on the ground, hold him quietly, and hand him off to Jeanne. Then I was supposed to keep the protective mother away while Jeanne tagged the calf. It's more than putting a tag in the calf's ear; Jeanne gives the newborn two shots of vitamins, puts iodine on the umbilical cord, and if it's a bull calf, puts a band around the scrotum that gradually castrates him.

Cows that have recently given birth have a special behavior; they go off by themselves and are very watchful and protective. Jeanne spotted one such cow, Cow 703.

"You'll have one chance to catch this one," Jeanne said as we approached the sleeping calf.

I hopped out of the truck and quickly approached the calf. As I did, the cow lunged forward at me to protect her baby. Unbeknownst to me, Jeanne realized this was a mean cow and had gotten out of the truck with her cow stick.

As I was running from the raging cow, Jeanne proceeded to smack the cow with the stick. Her backswing with the stick hit me right on the head. The front swing hit the cow. Luckily the cow tripped on her baby, which gave us a split second to escape into the cab of the truck.

"Well, what do we do now?" I asked as we both gasped for air.

"We rope him," Jeanne replied.

"You drive, and I'll get on the back with the rope."

Jeanne gave me explicit instructions as I drove toward the pair running away from us. "Faster!" she said. "Get closer!"

I thought it was an ungodly speed and that I would run over the calf. In a split-second Jeanne leaned over from the bed of the pickup and dispatched a large loop in the rope around the head and chest of the running calf and cinched it tight.

With the jerk of the rope the calf immediately dropped to the ground, which made the cow even more incensed.

I stopped the truck and slung myself through the window and onto the bed of the pickup to help Jeanne pull the calf onto the bed. All the while, the fuming mad cow was running around the truck and crashing into its sides.

As I held the calf down, Jeanne gave him two shots of vitamins, banded his scrotum, iodined his navel, and put a tag in his ear. She picked up the two rear legs, I got the front ones, and we lowered the calf onto the ground.

The mean mother was all over the calf. Jeanne and I scrambled back into the cab through the windows and drove off to leave them alone.

I thought, "Now this is one tough woman."

Love Story on the Middle River

Jeanne Trimble Hoffman is a beef cattle farmer. I am a soil and water conservationist. Many years ago, we fell in love, and in 2004 we married.

Can you imagine the dance, with our values, during our courtship years? What resulted is amazing. And now fourteen years after we tied the knot, we not only love each other more than ever, one can actually see the blending of our values in the way we farm.

Jeanne is a very hard-working, fast-paced, work-till-you-drop farmer. She can ride any horse and rope a calf from a horse or from the back of a pickup truck. She can drive a tractor, a hydra-bed, and a bull. She also fenced the cows out of all the streams on her farm and put the farm under an open-space conservation easement.

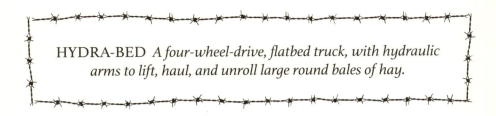

HYDRA-BED *A four-wheel-drive, flatbed truck, with hydraulic arms to lift, haul, and unroll large round bales of hay.*

Jeanne's farm is in America's legendary Shenandoah Valley, in the western part of Virginia. This valley is flanked on the west by the Allegheny Mountains and on the east by the Blue Ridge Mountains. Within this valley of rolling hills is a small, rural community in Augusta County called Swoope (rhymes with hope). Most of the soils here are deep and well drained. We receive enough rain to grow our crops without irrigation. That's why this valley was a sacred hunting ground for Native Americans and the Breadbasket of the Confederacy—it can grow a lot of food. It remains the most productive farmland in Virginia.

The Middle River, a tributary of the South Fork of the Shenandoah, flows through this farm for a half mile. Two unnamed tributaries are born here; they just seep out of the ground and flow to the river.

Jeanne is a ninth-generation farmer. That's one of the reasons I call her the Princess of Swoope. Her family has been farming this same land since 1746 when her ancestor John Trimble purchased the land from William Beverley, the proprietor of the Beverley Manor Land Grant. Trimble's Mill operated on the banks of the Middle River until it was torn down in the 2000s. We live on Trimbles Mill Road.

The Middle River, born just six miles upstream, is perhaps the most polluted river in Augusta County. It's on Virginia's Impaired Waters List because it violates two state standards for water quality: *E. coli* and sediment. It's polluted because of all the cattle that are allowed to freely roam in the river and its tributaries.

Jeanne's farm is an example of how agriculture and conservation can work together as one, just like a good marriage. In the beginning, Jeanne wanted more grass, and I wanted more riparian buffer. Now, fourteen years after our marriage and fourteen years after we fenced the cows out of the river, we can see that our marriage and the way we farm are truly a blending of our values and respect for each other.

We can honestly say that this farm produces food and clean water.

I sample the river for *E. coli* for the Friends of Middle River. The state standard for *E. coli* in freshwater streams is 235 colony-forming units per 100 milliliters of water. This is represented as 235 cfu/100 mL. When the river enters the farm, the *E. coli* counts are consistently over 1,000 cfu/100 mL. When the river leaves the farm after it travels only a half mile, the *E. coli* counts are reduced on average by fifty-five percent.

Why? There are several reasons. First, cows no longer make direct discharges of manure and urine into the waterways on this farm. Second, dilution from additional water comes from low-flow groundwater sources and two intermittent streams on our farm. Maybe sunlight has a small part. But the most important factor is the riparian forest buffer. The streamside forest supplies leaves that feed an emerging aquatic ecosystem that processes in-stream pollution.

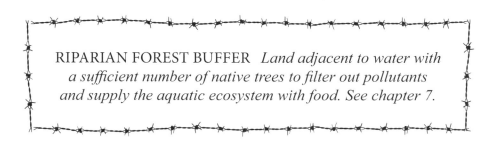

RIPARIAN FOREST BUFFER *Land adjacent to water with a sufficient number of native trees to filter out pollutants and supply the aquatic ecosystem with food. See chapter 7.*

We cannot have clean water without healthy farmland, and healthy farmland is achieved by installing best management practices to the land. Riparian buffers, bioengineering practices to stabilize eroding banks, stream exclusion of livestock, and rotational grazing all work together to produce clean water, pollinator corridors, and food.

Jeanne believes in protecting the farm forever. She placed a conservation easement on the property in 2005 that extinguished any right to subdivide the property. This will be a farm forever. It is here where we continue our dance of combined values and respect for the land and water.

Aaron Bophum

Our truck was in the shop, so Jeanne drove me over to Meade Shuey's to borrow our old farm truck to feed the cows. Two of the tires looked a little low on air. My job was to put air in the tires and feed the herd of cows in the back field.

As I was coming out of the back field after feeding a bale of hay, Jeanne asked, "Got Aaron Bophum?"

"Huh?" I replied.

"Got Aaron Bophum?" she yelled.

"Who's he?" I replied.

"Jesus, mother of God. I can't believe you don't know what I'm saying," she exclaimed. "Do. You. Have Air. In. Both. Of. Them?"

Calving Season Begins March 1

Green grass emerges from its brown, dormant cloak of winter. Northern Harriers glide and teeter close to the ground in search of anything that moves. In the vast grasslands of Swoope, Virginia, the headwaters of the Shenandoah River, they hunt voles. American Plum pushes forth its white blooms, and the metallic blue, white-bellied Tree Swallows arrive to guard nesting sites for their mates. This is March, the beginning of calving season on our beef cattle farm.

We have 138 pregnant beef cows this year that will give birth beginning around March first. It is absolutely the busiest time of the year on the farm, and most days and nights in March we must be on alert, around the clock. Seventy percent of the calves are born during the first thirty days of the month.

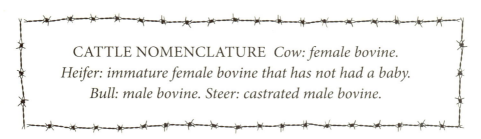

CATTLE NOMENCLATURE *Cow: female bovine. Heifer: immature female bovine that has not had a baby. Bull: male bovine. Steer: castrated male bovine.*

We divide the mature cows into two groups, and we have one group of first-calf heifers; this year we have twenty-five heifers. We contain them in the small fields near the house so we can keep close watch on them during labor and the birthing process. Half of them will need some sort of assistance because it is their first birth. They can be unpredictable, from being dumb to freaking out, screaming, and head-butting their baby.

Jeanne, in my opinion, is a cow whisperer. She's hard-driving, with little patience. But when it comes to calves, her patience emerges. She can think like a cow. One time I saw a cow dip her head at Jeanne and start charging. I would have run. But not Jeanne; she charged the cow! And sure enough, the cow went the other way. All this and pearl earrings too. As I said, the Princess of Swoope.

Inevitably, a storm or a blizzard arrives during every calving season, and we try to prepare for it. If a calf dies, we blame ourselves for lack of attention or endurance. I remember one year we had a snow-blowing blizzard during a full moon; nine calves were born and four perished from exposure before we could get to them. To this day we still blame ourselves.

This year, Winter Storm Stella brought arctic cold wind and subzero temperatures during a full moon. We were lucky,

> **EAR TAG NUMBERING LOGIC** *A calf's ear tag is the same number as its mother's. Cow ear tags have a roman or arabic numeral to identify the year the calf was born. Cows and calves with red and yellow ear tags are Jeanne's. All other cows and calves, most of which have white tags but some of which have green, belong to Jean. I still get confused with the Hoffman Farms numbering system.*

receiving only two inches of snow as opposed to eleven that had been forecast. This is when we "farmer-up." The cold was not going to take a single baby from us if we could help it.

March 14

7:30 p.m. We checked the cows in the back field group. It is dark, snowing, and twenty-six degrees, with a howling wind making the chill far below zero. Cow X2's baby is shivering on the ground. It is cold to the touch. Jeanne puts her finger in its mouth: barely warm. We pick up the calf and carry him to the back of the Jeep. Jeanne's old mail Jeep is a perfect calf carrier. I call it Uber for calves.

With the hatch open, I sit in the back of the jeep with the cold, wet calf on my lap. Jeanne drives slowly toward the barn while making a sick calf call; the mother follows in a panicked kind of way. I watch her bulging eyes and the breath shooting out of both nostrils as she follows. She smells her baby, screams a little, and then follows. A couple of times the cow puts her head in the Jeep. Her head appears much larger than normal as she smells my face, looking for her baby.

A few times she gets confused and runs around the Jeep. We stop, set the baby out on the ground, let the pair reconnect, then get back into the Jeep and head to the barn.

At the barn, Jeanne opens the gates, and I carry the calf to what we call the porch. It's an extension of the barn with a roof and two sides. It will be much warmer there and the pair can be out of the wind and bond in private.

March 15

10:30 p.m. We check the Wheatlands group. Cow 125 calved, and the baby is cold to the touch. It will probably not survive the subzero temperatures. We pick him up, put him in the Jeep, and return to the barn, leaving his mother alone in the dark. We put the calf into the "calf cooker"—actually a calf warmer. It looks like a big lunchbox with a heater in it. His mother will be okay but miserable, looking for him all night.

We don't see any additional cows with calving behavior, so we go to the house for some rest. Lying in bed while Jeanne sleeps, I worry about whether I put the heater in the calf cooker on too hot a setting.

Tomorrow we may have pot roast.

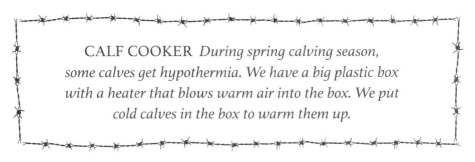

CALF COOKER *During spring calving season, some calves get hypothermia. We have a big plastic box with a heater that blows warm air into the box. We put cold calves in the box to warm them up.*

5 a.m. Thirteen degrees and strong wind. We suit up in coveralls, boots, coats, and gloves. The moon lights our way to the barn. The ground crunches as we walk. Filled with anxiety, we hope the baby in the cooker is alive. We peek into the cooker, and presto! the little guy is standing up and gives us a loud good morning: "Baaaa! I want my mother!"

Jeanne and I take the baby to its mother in the Wheatlands field. It's not quite pitch dark, thanks to the full moon, so we drive with no headlights. We assume she, as a good mother, will be in the same spot where she calved. She is.

We drop the baby off right in front of her, and they immediately hook up.

During the rest of the morning, two more cold babies go into the cooker to warm up. It's like a revolving door on this frigid day.

1 p.m. Jeanne and Bob (our helper during calving) see Cow 414 is in labor. One foot out and a nose. Where is the other foot? A foot back is really bad. Both mother and baby may die unless assisted. They walk her into the barnyard and into the long narrow passage to the head catch. Once the cow's head is locked in place, Jeanne goes into the womb with her arm, finds the leg that's bent back, brings it forward alongside the other leg, and puts calf-obstetric chains around the two feet. I'm holding the cow's tail while Jeanne and Bob are in the chute directly behind the cow. They attach handles to the chains and gently pull the legs when the cow pushes during a contraction. It's an easy pull. The warm calf comes out and they carry it to the adjacent pen.

We are sad and bewildered. The calf is dead. Could we have done more? Was it our fault? The cow wasn't in labor that long; it was an easy pull. What happened? That calf should not have died. Where did we fail? We will never know, and we will live with that guilt for a long time.

The mama cow licks the dead baby dry trying to make it live, not understanding. We all know what must be done: graft another calf onto this mother.

As we continue checking cows and calves in the subzero temperatures, Jeanne gets on the phone to our beef cattle neighbors to see if anyone has a twin or orphan calf they want to sell.

We called all our beef cattle friends to see if they had any bottle babies they could sell. No extra babies are available now because of the weather. Any beef cattle farmer that had a twin would want to keep it in this weather in case they needed one to graft onto one of

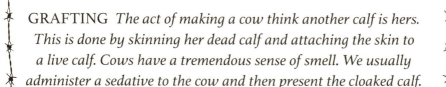

GRAFTING *The act of making a cow think another calf is hers. This is done by skinning her dead calf and attaching the skin to a live calf. Cows have a tremendous sense of smell. We usually administer a sedative to the cow and then present the cloaked calf.*

their cows. We go to great lengths to obtain a baby because the cow has milk and wants a baby.

When no beef cattle babies are available, we resort to dairy calves. I call my friend Keith at Cave View Dairy in Weyers Cave to see if he has any babies for sale. Bingo! He has one.

3 p.m. Jeanne feeds hay to the herds with the tractor. Bob drags the dead 414 baby to the other side of the barn and hangs it from an iron hook to skin it. He leaves the umbilical cord and tail intact with the skin. I put our Border Collie, Val, in the jeep and drive to Weyers Cave to get the dairy calf.

Keith meets me at their maternity barn. It's a five-day-old, castrated, Holstein bull calf. Keith helps me lift the big black-and-white calf into the back of the Jeep. The calf stands up in the back and remains fairly calm. His back touches the ceiling of the Jeep.

"Well, are you going to tie him up or anything?" asks Keith.
My mind flashes back to other beef calves I have picked up for this purpose, which was like wrestling with a billy goat in a small cage.

"No, he'll be alright," I reply.

Val looks at the calf. I guess to him it looks like a giant Border Collie. He sneaks into the footwell of the passenger seat, curls up, and hides his head between his paws.

Off we go. The bull calf stands up during the entire forty-five-minute drive back to the farm. He would make a great sailor with that kind of balance.

Meanwhile, Heifer 152 has just had her baby, so Jeanne and Bob put the pair in the barn on the porch. The mother will lick that baby warm.

Uber for calves arrives at the barn. Bob and I put the dairy calf in the center room of the barn and tie the black Angus skin from the dead calf on him with baler twine.

5:30 p.m. Jeanne moves the 414 cow into the chute. As the cow walks down the chute I place a four-foot-long pipe behind her in front of the posts in the chute to prevent her from backing up. Jeanne walks behind the cow in the chute with a syringe of magic drugs that will make her go to la-la land for a while. She gives the shot as the cow walks down the chute into the head catch.

Bob and I walk the Holstein calf wearing his new skin in front of the cow in the head catch. She takes several deep smells and gives out a cow's motherly sound. It's the "Oh my God, it's my baby," sound. Once we hear that sound, we know it's going to work. Jeanne places the calf alongside the cow with his head near the udder, and, wow, the calf starts nursing immediately. The cow makes more cooing sounds.

We release the cow from the head catch and put the two in the pen next to the chute to let nature take its course. That dairy calf nurses for all he's worth. He's much taller than a beef cattle baby, so he has to turn his head sideways to nurse. He nurses her on his knees. He nurses her when she is lying down. He has hit the "mother lode"!

7:30 p.m. Back to the calving fields we go. It's still below zero and windy.

Only a strong newborn calf and a good mother can survive in this kind of weather. In the back field, Cow 44 had her baby. It is up, dry, and nursing; they will be fine. On to the Wheatlands field. As we drive in, I see a Bald Eagle fly over the pasture in front of us with the snow-covered mountains in the background. The eagle is carrying a large stick in its talons for nesting material.

The moment concluded another day during calving season. We both feel so fortunate to be farmers and to be living in such a beautiful place. Even though the days are long sometimes, it makes us appreciate the hard work of all farmers. We don't think of it as work but rather as a chosen way of life.

Volvos or Vulvas?

Our new neighbors had never seen a calf being born. One evening one of our cows in the barnyard went into labor; her water bag had burst. We called Doug and Sally to come over and watch the birth. We set up lounge chairs, had a glass of wine, and began to watch.

We watched and waited . . . watched and waited. It was dark; nothing happened. Jeanne decided to "go in." That meant putting the cow in the chute, trapping her head in the head catch and going into the womb to find out what's going on.

Imagine getting a black cow into the chute in the dark . . . .

After much consternation and yelling we managed to get the cow into the head catch, and Jeanne instructed me to get some water from the spring to wash the cow's posterior end.

As I swiftly walked to the spring with a bucket Sally asked what I was doing. Sally is from England, so imagine this conversation in her English dialect and my southern one.

"I'm getting some water to wash the vulva," I said.

"Volvo, I don't see a Volvo," she replied.

I couldn't see Doug for the darkness, but he said, "No, Sally, we wash Volvos; they wash vulvas!"

My First Horse

Jeanne loves horses. She's been riding since she was four. I *reeaally* liked this woman, so I thought it would be cool if I had a horse to ride with her. Well, it just so happened there was a five-state Quarter Horse sale in Abingdon, Virginia, coming up in a couple months. The sale list was online. Jeanne and I researched all the horses and narrowed it down to three horses that we both liked. The number one horse on our list was Whiskey's Playtoy. The second on the list was Mr. Lightning Flash. I can't remember the third horse's name, but it had some sort of fast-paced ring to it.

We arrived the night before the sale to look at the horses we picked out or maybe find another one just right for me—a dead broke, easy keeper.

We found Whiskey's Playtoy. A gorgeous horse. People were all around making a bunch of noise, and the horse was calm—we thought this would be the horse for me.

The owner, a big, barrel-chested, very nice cowboy, said I could come by early in the morning to test ride him.

We arrived at eight o'clock the next morning. The indoor arena was as big as a football field. Sawdust covered the ground. The cowboy was waiting for us. We said morning niceties, and then he said I could go ahead and get on the horse.

I was very nervous. I put my left foot in the stirrup, hands on the saddle horn, and gently pulled myself up, being careful to sit down gently. As soon as I sat quietly on the horse, and I mean at that instant, he took off like a rocket. I held on for dear life with every muscle I had. Legs, arms, feet—anything I had to hold on to I gripped, which is the exact opposite of how to stop a horse. I was actually telling the horse to go fast by gripping with my legs. The harder I gripped the faster he went.

Sawdust was flying, and I could see people running away in my peripheral vision.

I heard the cowboy ask Jeanne, "What's his name, ma'am?"

"Bobby," she said.

The cowboy called out to me, "Bobby, relax... relax." As soon as I relaxed, the horse stopped.

Oh my God. This horse had pushbuttons all over him. He was way too much horse for me, but Jeanne got on and had a fabulous time.

The next horse we tried was Mr. Lightning Flash. He was a nice horse with a good eye. You knew when you looked into his eye that he was kind. He was a beautiful paint horse. Jeanne and I both rode him and were pleased.

We made a deal outside the arena, and my sister Lynn let us use her trailer to get him home.

Grass Tetany Took Her Life

After three vet visits and gentle care from all of us, the decision was made to put her down.

She was a good cow, 400, one of those big old Charolaise cows with a sweet disposition, delivering a good calf every year without any problems—the kind of sweet cow every farmer would love to have. She was born here in 1994. In this, her final year, she had twins. She was killed by a lack of magnesium in her body, a condition called grass tetany.

After she twinned, she retained part of her placenta, so we had to get her into the chute, clean her, and make sure both calves were nursing. She never found the salt in the barnyard that had the magnesium in it, which would have saved her.

I grieved and said a prayer before shooting her. When the deed was done, we put chains around her hind legs and dragged her body through the back pasture to a grave on the hill.

A few days later we moved the herd she belonged to into the same pasture through which I had pulled her body.

Her herd mates, all forty of them, ran over to the path where I had dragged their fallen friend's body. Somehow, they knew. Some of them bawled, some bucked and kicked, some ran in circles. They knew ... and they grieved. And as I watched their grieving unfold before me, it made me cry.

The Chosen Ones

Our farming operation is almost a closed system. Although we sometimes buy calves from other farms, we never buy any breeding cows. They are all born here. The only new genetics to the farm come from the bulls we buy. We save the best female calves (heifers) to become breeder cows on the farm. The best heifers are the ones that come from well-mannered mothers, with good udders and feet. In November each year, we bring the herds into a small paddock where Jeanne and her mother Jean can pick out the heifers that will become legacy cows on Hoffman Farms.

I loaded the pickup truck with ten square bales of newly made alfalfa hay. The herd from the north was already in the small pasture surrounding the barn across the road we call the red barn. I took my knife and cut the strings on one of the bales. I lifted a few flakes of hay to my nose and breathed in the wonderful smell of well-made hay, it was sweet and earthy. I walked among the cows with these flakes of hay. It was like walking around with a pan of fresh brownies in a group of teenagers. The cows inched closer and stretched their heads toward the flakes of hay, sniffing wildly. A couple of sniffs and their tongues extended like hands grabbing as much as they could. It is amazing how much they can grab with their tongues. It is much more than a single mouthful. The cows stand there, encircling me, with these beards of hay extending for a couple of feet below their mouths; their tongues work in a circular motion to swiftly cram it all into their mouths. The sound of their chewing and breathing is all that I can hear.

While I'm doing this, Jean and Jeanne walked quietly through the herd, evaluating the calves to see which heifers they would keep to replace the older cows. It's quite an honor to be selected.

Cattle Drive on the Public Roads

On Hoffman Farms, we keep the first-time-pregnant heifers at Jeanne's mother's place, which is three miles from our home at Meadowview. We usually hire local people with trailers to haul them to the barnyard at Meadowview a couple of weeks before they are due to calve.

One year, there was a snowstorm, and cold weather had set in. Trucks that haul cattle couldn't get into Jean's because of the deep snow, so Jeanne organized a cattle drive to move the heifers the three miles from Jean's to the barnyard at Meadowview. They would have to walk on the public roads. At 1:50 p.m. I opened the gate at Jean's to let thirty-nine pregnant heifers onto Glebe School Road. All our friends and neighbors were helping by standing at yards or roads so the cows wouldn't wander off the road. I drove the hydra-bed with Jeanne on the back calling them. She had a few bales of really good hay to entice them to follow.

Jean and Bob were in the brown truck behind the cows to keep them moving. As we passed neighbors and friends along the way, they would wave and take pictures. It was an hour-and-fifteen-minute cattle parade. Cars pulled off the road and people waved. The whole community helped us out. We were very thankful for them.

The Calf Was Coming Out Backward

At about 2 p.m. Jeanne and I went to feed and check the cows. I put on my binocular harness so we could have ten-power vision.

When we crested the hill in the back field, Jeanne saw a calf's hoof protruding from Y85's vulva. I trained the binoculars on her and saw that the foot was "toe up," which meant the calf was coming out backward.

Calves rarely survive a backward delivery, and sometimes both mother and baby die. We had to move quickly.

Jeanne called Bob, who, lucky for us, was just leaving the farm. We got all the cows into the barnyard with the lure of some good hay. Once all the cows were in, we sorted Y85 away and put her into the chute. This all happened within a few minutes and without any talking.

I got the calving chains and gave them to Jeanne, and then I jumped into the chute behind her to help pull. After she put the chains around the hind feet of the calf, we both pulled in rhythm with the cow's contractions. The legs emerged easily, but we were not strong enough to hand pull past the buttocks of the calf, so Bob went to get the calf jack. This is a metal pole about eight feet long with a come-a-long attached that you brace against the cow, enabling you to pull the calf.

We braced the jack up to the rear of the cow and hooked the chains, which were still attached to the calf's feet, to the cable on the jack. I began to crank the cable. Bob held the cow's tail to the side and just as the buttocks of the calf cleared, the cow wailed at the top of her lungs and a large amount of soupy manure exited the cow's anus under such intense pressure that it covered the whole spectrum of vision.

I saw this in slow motion. A geyser of manure. A fire hose of warm, green manure first hit Jeanne directly in the face, and then it hit me. Even as Jeanne was getting sprayed, she was shouting, "CRANK!" telling me to pull the cable. The high-pressure manure went right into her mouth. Of course, she turned her head and the manure went right into her ear. Jeanne was in high-energy mode, spitting the manure out of her mouth and yelling for me to crank in between spits and curse words.

I cranked and cranked until there was no more cable to crank. We then put downward pressure on the pole of the jack and the calf's head emerged. The entire seventy-pound calf dropped to the chute floor amid all the water-bag fluid and manure.

To our sheer delight the calf was alive!

We hung him upside-down over the fence by his hind legs to drain his lungs. When he was breathing well, we let him down in the pen next to the chute.

We let the poor cow out of the head catch, and she immediately went to licking and talking to her baby. We all smiled in relief and exhaustion. Bob and I both looked at our manure-soaked leader, who even had manure on her pearl earrings. She began to cautiously chuckle, and then she started laughing, and we all had a good hearty laugh.

Jeanne Skis Behind the Cow

Cow 93 needed help delivering her calf, so Jeanne and I put her in the chute and captured her in the head catch. Jean and Bob arrived. Jeanne had the chains around the calf's front feet, and she and I were pulling in rhythm with the mother's contractions.

The mother was making signs of lying down in the chute, something you never want to happen while you are pulling the calf. Jeanne yelled to her mother: "GET THE COW UP!"

Jean mistook that as "Let the cow out," as in, open the head catch.

Jean pulled the lever to open the head catch.

Oh my God. The cow took off like a bull in a rodeo, with Jeanne and me holding on for dear life to the chains still attached to the legs of the calf emerging from the womb. Jeanne slid across the chute floor on her butt and I slid on my knees, both of us holding onto the calving chains. I let go after about twenty feet and watched

Jeanne skiing on her butt behind the racing cow cursing as she slid through the barnyard.

She finally let go of the handle on the chain. Jeanne was livid. The cow was rattled, now with her baby's feet protruding from womb with chains still attached to the feet. Patience was required to get the cow back into the chute to finish the job. The calf was alive when it finally arrived, and the mother accepted her baby with ease.

Mixed-Up Twins

Yesterday before Jeanne went to work, we watched Cow 503; something just didn't seem right. She acted as if she wanted to go into labor but never did; this is rather typical of a breech baby (one that is backward in the womb). We put her in the head catch to find out what was going on. Jeanne put on an arm-length latex glove and went into the womb to check it out. In a normal delivery, you would feel two front feet and a head. Instead, she felt four front feet—twins were on the way, but in this case the feet were tangled up, and both twins were trying to come out at the same time, causing the cow's aberrant behavior and preventing delivery. Jeanne immediately called the vet, knowing she was in over her head. She then left for work, leaving Jean and me to tend to the cow with the vet.

The vet arrived about ten minutes later. He is in his seventies with a gray crewcut that looks like he cuts it himself. He shaves his beard maybe once a week, so sometimes the whiskers on his face are as long as the hairs on his head. He's a short, stocky, gruff, hairy guy reminding me of an old sailor on Blackbeard's pirate ship.

He unzipped his coveralls down to his navel and took his right arm out of the sleeve. I was amazed at all the shoulder and arm hair. He put a latex glove on his right arm that went all the way to his armpit and then put some gel on his gloved arm to make it slick before sticking his arm into the womb of the cow. When the vet's head is near the cow's anus, it is customary for someone to hold the cow's tail away from his head, so Jean was performing this task. While the vet was investigating the entangled twins, Jean informed him that this was our thirteenth set of twins this year. Actually, it was only our seventh, but I've learned, as son-in-law, that it wouldn't be prudent for me to comment, especially in this situation. But to myself I was thinking how comical it all was and secretly smiled while trying to hold back what I was dying to say.

The vet felt around for what seemed like a whole five minutes, feeling and making grunting noises that doctors make when they're thinking.

"What do you think, Doc?" I asked.

"It's a mess," he grumbled.

The chains went in, and after he and I pulled and then released several times we put the handles on the chains and pulled until two feet appeared, then a nose. We then attached the chains to the calf jack, cranked a few times, and the first baby came out alive. We went in for the second one and he came out alive as well. The mother took both babies. It would be a good day.

The Lame Bull and Bova Glue

One of our bulls is lame. We knew he was lame on the ninth of August but thought his injury would heal on its own in a few days. It didn't, so we called the vet. We couldn't get the bull up, so the vet tranquilized the bull where he lay so he could investigate the lame foot. In addition to tranquilizing the bull, we tied his head to his rear leg to help immobilize him.

Bovines have cloven hooves—two clawlike structures on each foot. The vet found an abscess on one of the claws on the bull's left hind foot. The doctor who came on this day was new to the area, and very young. He said he was going to glue a block of wood onto the good claw of the lame foot so when the bull walked, the bad claw wouldn't get any pressure; thus allowing it to heal.

"Wow," I thought, "he's going to glue a block of wood onto a two-thousand-pound mass of testosterone."

Even John, the next-door neighbor, came over to the edge of the fence to watch the operation. As he leaned on the fence smoking a cigarette, he chuckled and mused, "You gonna glue a block of wood onto the bull's foot?"

The young vet used a double-barreled epoxy gun to apply "bova glue" to the block of wood and the bull's toe. He wore gloves and was not having much success at all so Jeanne offered to help, but she only succeeded in getting glue all over herself. It took days for that stuff to come off.

The block of wood fell off the next day, and we found out the bull was lame in the other foot as well. We had to water and feed the bull twice a day. In addition, we had to administer antibiotics.

A bull weighing a ton required 108 ccs of medicine in eleven different sites, every day for five days. He was walking now but still far from healed. We didn't really know how we were going to confine him for eleven shots because we don't have a head catch large enough for a bull's head.

Jeanne said we would just walk behind him and give him the eleven shots. My job was to hold his tail, but oh my God, the bull was up and moving. I grabbed his tail, and of course he didn't like that too much. Then Jeanne thrust the needle into his butt, and things got moving a little faster. The three of us were travelling across the field. He kept throwing his five-hundred-pound head from side to side to get me off his tail. We zig-zagged all over that field. Jeanne instructed me to just stay behind him . . . just stay behind him. The bull was snorting and swaying back and forth. There I was, holding the tail of a two-thousand-pound bull that didn't like it at all. Jeanne was a real trooper. She gave him the eleven shots, and we both lived.

The bull finally got well enough to walk onto a trailer so we sent him to the stockyard on October 5.

Feeding the Heifers on Frozen Ground

This day in late November, we started feeding hay in earnest. We got up early to feed at Jean's to take advantage of the frozen ground. You have to feed on frozen ground during wet periods because if you wait until the ground thaws, the truck will get stuck.

So, at daylight and twenty-three degrees, Jeanne drove me and Dexter, our Border Collie at the time, in the hydra-bed down to Jean's place. There we picked up a large round bale of hay and entered the meadow where the heifers were. The hungry heifers were eager for the food; they ran toward us as soon as I opened the gate, twirling and bucking as they ran. Imagine a thousand-pound bovine pirouette. After we took the net wrap off the bale, Jeanne rolled out a few turns of the dried hay and then put the remainder in the round bale feeder.

We drove about twenty yards and then stopped to look back at the heifers. Every single cow was eating the rolled-out hay. I love to see the hay dangling from their chewing mouths. The morning air was thick with moisture, and you could easily hear them chewing and breathing. You could see their breath and the vapor rising off their frost-covered backs. At that moment, the sun rose. What a beautiful day.

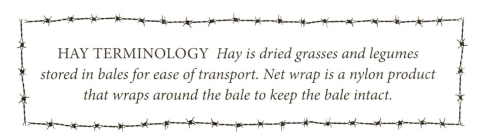

HAY TERMINOLOGY *Hay is dried grasses and legumes stored in bales for ease of transport. Net wrap is a nylon product that wraps around the bale to keep the bale intact.*

As we looked back, we both noticed a bit of hay that was left on the back of the flatbed of the truck. Usually one of us gets out to sweep it off with an arm, so I asked my dear wife, "Darling, you want me to get that hay off the truck?"

"No, I'll get it off," she replied.

At that moment, she stomped on the accelerator. The G-force slammed Dexter and me against the back seat, and the remnant of hay was left in the field for the cows.

"I love life!" she laughed, as we exited the field.

The Vet Tied Cow Y911 Shut

The Y911 cow was in labor. Last year, she had a uterine prolapse. After she delivered her baby, her entire uterus came out. It was about the size of a small refrigerator. There she was, lying down and licking her baby. On the ground behind her lay her uterus still attached. It was so sad.

The vet put a huge stainless-steel pan under the uterus. He cleaned and rinsed it with saline water and then slowly pushed it back in where it was supposed to be. He sewed her vulva shut with some sort of surgical string to keep the uterus from coming back out. A job well done.

As he drove off he said, "If she's alive in the morning, give me a call."

She lived! And got pregnant. And now, a year later, she was in labor. We all feared she would have another prolapse so we put her in with the heifers so we could keep a close eye on her.

We gave her fifteen minutes. Only one of her calf's feet was protruding out of the vulva about ten inches, which was unusual. Jeanne told me to go to the barn and get the head catch ready.

I ran to the head catch, but then Jeanne screamed for me to come quick. She was crying and in anguish screaming, "He tied her shut! He tied her shut!"

The poor cow was lying there, trying in vain to push her baby out. The vet who put her uterus back in had sewed her womb shut with permanent material.

Jeanne's adrenaline kicked in. She yelled for me to get a knife, so I raced to the kitchen to get one. Meanwhile, Jeanne made the cow get up and walked her into the chute. She cut the stitches before the heifer even got to the head catch. Then Jeanne put the calving chains on the hooves of the calf. We both pulled at the moment the mother was pushing, and the calf came out. The baby was alive!

Jeanne Roped the Calf from the Hood of the Truck

It was raining and seventy-two degrees. We went to tag the 01 baby in the Wheatlands field. The cow was so mean, though, that Jeanne had to rope the calf from the hood of the truck. That's right: she got on the hood of the truck, I drove, and she roped the calf from the hood. As soon as she cinched the rope around the calf, I put the truck in park, climbed out the window, and helped Jeanne pull the calf onto the hood. After we did the usual banding, gave it two shots of vitamins, put iodine on its navel, and tagged its ear, we slid the calf off the truck's hood and back onto the ground.

We got back into the truck by way of the windows and continued our rounds of chores.

Calf X8, Broken Leg, Cat Food Bag, and Grady

Calf X8 was a big Charolaise baby. So big we had to assist the cow in delivery by pulling with the jack. In the process one of his legs broke. A few moments after the delivery, the mother died. One of her arteries in the uterus hemorrhaged and she bled to death.

Sadly, there was nothing we could do.

The vet came and put a full cast on the right front leg of Calf X8. We now had a baby that we would give a bottle of replacer milk to three times a day.

Several days later the B2 calf died. It was breech. The mother wanted a calf so we thought we would graft the X8 bottle baby onto the B2 cow.

Bob skinned the dead calf and I helped him tie the hide onto the X8 calf. Jeanne gave the cow drugs to make the transition easier. It was drizzling rain so we needed something to keep X8's cast dry. I went to the house frantically looking for something and settled for an empty cat food bag. It was a comical situation. There we were trying to graft this white calf with black skin tied on him, his broken leg in a cast with a cat food bag taped onto the end. The poor cow. She's going to need a lot of drugs to accept this calf.

Jean was there watching the situation unfold. Jeanne told me her mother's car battery had died, so I tried to have a conversation with her.

"Did you get a battery for your car?" I asked Jean.

"Yes," she replied, "I went to Advance Auto to get a battery. They only had six-, seven-, and eight-year-old batteries. I told them I didn't want one that old."

Puzzled, I said, "You mean you didn't want one to last that long?"

"Yes," she answered, "I said I didn't want to have the car that long and wanted a two- or three-year-old battery. They told me to go to Walmart."

One month later...

Calf X8 has had a very unusual life so far. We call him Grady now. His cast is off, and he seems to be healthy except he doesn't have a mother. Jeanne loves on him every chance she gets. We tried to graft him onto three cows, all to no avail. Then one day a Charolaise cow, G8, had her calf. Her teats were so big her own calf couldn't get ahold of them to nurse. They were so big I thought if you touched them they would explode. In cow speak they call this balloon teat. Jeanne's ingenuity kicked in. She got the cow in the chute, trapped her in the head catch and then milked her by hand until she thought Grady could nurse. I brought Grady to her and he went to town sucking those huge teats. After Grady milked her down and was full, he stepped back and started walking around. He teetered to the right, then to the left as if he was drunk. He looked really full. He staggered and farted every step he took.

Jeanne put the cow in the shoot every day for weeks to hand milk and let Grady have a meal. The G8 cow had enough milk for both Grady and her own calf. Grady now lives happily on a neighbor's farm.

Thankful to Be a Farmer

This afternoon, I picked up our dear friend Dr. H. Bruce Rinker at his home to bring him out to the farm for several hours. We rode through the herds of cattle to see the newborns and make sure they were okay. As we were riding through a pasture he asked me, "Do you think of this as a chore every day, or do you see it as a wonder every day?"

It made me appreciate, once again, how lucky I am to be here and to be with Jeanne, the most remarkable woman I have ever known: hard working, intelligent, caring, and so beautiful. Her leadership and her love for the animals makes the farm successful and such a joy.

I don't consider our work here on the farm as work. It is our life, and I feel so lucky to be in it. So many things just amaze me every day, like the birth of a calf in cold weather, seeing a clutch of Killdeer scuttling from us as we drive the truck through the pasture with hay, or just looking at Jeanne in her farm clothes and pearl earrings.

Jeanne calling the cows; now that's very special. I so enjoy her calling the cows, every single day. And I enjoy seeing Val's tail fluffed up when he is excited. Val is our two-year-old Border Collie. His tail

looks like a white pom-pom on top of his body.
    Here are a few things I love:
    Jeanne calling the cows
    Val's excited, fluffy white tail
    A Bald Eagle perched on a snag
    Tree Swallows hovering over their nest box
    Heat from the woodstove
    The smell of good hay
    Cows jumping up and down at good hay
    Bobwhites calling
    The kind eye of a horse
    A newborn calf finding his mother
    Daffodils in bloom
    My grandson hitting upside-down pots with spoons
    Tomatoes on the vine
    Fresh corn on the cob with butter and salt
    Green grass and big, white, puffy clouds against
        a brilliant blue sky
    Rain in May
    Jeanne gathering flowers to give away
    Hummingbirds gathering nectar from Jewelweed
        at the river
    Mayflies hatching over a clean stream
    A full sail on a broad reach
    The smell of rich soil
    Truth
    Children singing
    A smiling face
    Snuggling with Jeanne
    Being with my kids
    My dad saying, "I love you too, son."

Does a Dead Cow Fit in Your Program?

A neighbor called to inform Jeanne that he had a cow that had not delivered her afterbirth and asked what could be done.

"We'll be right over," she told him.

When we arrived, he had put the cow in a stall with a small stanchion. We helped him move the cow into the stanchion to catch her head. Jeanne put on an arm-length surgical glove and then put her arm into the womb. It had been days since the cow had given birth so the afterbirth had a putrid odor.

Jeanne proceeded to remove the afterbirth. We brought uterine boluses to place inside the womb and penicillin to fight infection.

The neighbor objected to using the infection-fighting medicine, saying, "Ahhhh, Jeanne, those don't fit in my program."

"Where does a dead cow fit in your program?" Jeanne replied.

She administered the drugs.

Calving Season 2018

Thirty-eight cows have calved.

We get up before dawn. Our waking thoughts are outside, wondering if any cows had calved during the night's cold and wind and whether the cows were good mothers. Good mothers lick their babies dry to keep them warm and present their udders in a calm way so that the babies find the nourishing teat that will keep them alive.

This day would turn out to be the most dramatic day so far this calving season.

We tagged three calves before 9 a.m. Everything looked normal. Everyone is alive and well. The calves run and jump around. I love it when they kangaroo jump around their mothers. I see a calf take off running like a deer, his mother chasing after him.

At about 10 a.m., Cow X12 had a baby, and it never got up. We think it was breech. We took it to Westwood Animal Hospital.

Dr. CJ, one of our veterinarians, came out to the Jeep where the newborn lay. She opened his mouth to look at his gums.

"Oh dear," she said. "Purple gums."

We carried the calf into the small animal hospital and laid him on a stainless-steel table. They put a little cup over his nose to administer oxygen, then lowered him into a warm bath.

CJ took his temperature. Ninety-one degrees.

"I've never brought one back to life from a temperature lower than ninety-four," she said.

After they got him stabilized they put him in a heated stall and waited for a miracle. Jeanne and I returned to the farm to check for new babies and to haul hay out of one the barns.

Later that day we got the call, the X12 calf didn't make it.

We grafted a twin calf from a nearby farm onto the X12 cow.

Eight more babies were born on this day, including the Y4X6 calf. The mother didn't claim her baby so we took him into the barn and placed him in the calf cooker for the night. The next morning after he warmed up we took him back to his mother behind the house, and she was eager to accept him.

March 11

Fifty-one cows have calved.

The snow started just before daybreak.

The forecast was for two to four inches; it turned out to be eight.

Two calves were born this day: 509 and 61.

The 509 cow and calf did great. This is when you say, "Wow, I can't believe they can do this." Eight inches of blowing, whiteout snow and the baby is warm and tucked into the hay. A good mother and a strong calf is a winning combination.

Heifer 61 didn't do so well. She didn't lick the baby dry, and the baby got cold. I picked him up and carried him to the back of the Jeep. With the hatch open, I sat in the back with the cold calf on my lap so the mother would see him. Jeanne drove toward the barn and made the sounds of a pitiful calf in order to lure the mother cow. The mother followed us all the way to the barn.

We put the calf in the calf cooker and the cow in a nearby stall. After the baby got warm, we put the two together in a stall to bond. The mother made good sounds with her baby and licked him.

March 18

Seventy-four cows have calved, two sets of twins, two calf deaths (both from exposure), sixty-four to go.

We had to get Cow 115 into the barn. She had twins, and the babies just weren't getting enough milk, though she had a huge udder. While checking for newborns, we stole one twin, put him in the Jeep, and drove him to the barn. Next, we put a halter on the remaining twin and put him on my lap in the Jeep. We hoped the mother would follow us for half a mile through five fields to the barn.

With Jeanne making a sick calf sound and a little luck, we all arrived at the barn. After the cow settled down a bit, we put her in the head catch to investigate her udder. Her starboard teats were fine but her port side had a problem. The front teat was nothing but blood (she had mastitis) and the hind teat was empty. Jeanne milked out the infected quarter and administered antibiotics into the teat. We let the twins nurse her starboard side down, and then we supplemented them with a half bottle each of milk replacer.

I went to the river field to clean out a few nest boxes in the north tributary. Finally! Tree Swallows. I've been waiting for them for weeks.

They came from Florida and Cuba to nest here. When they get here, it's the first day of spring for me.

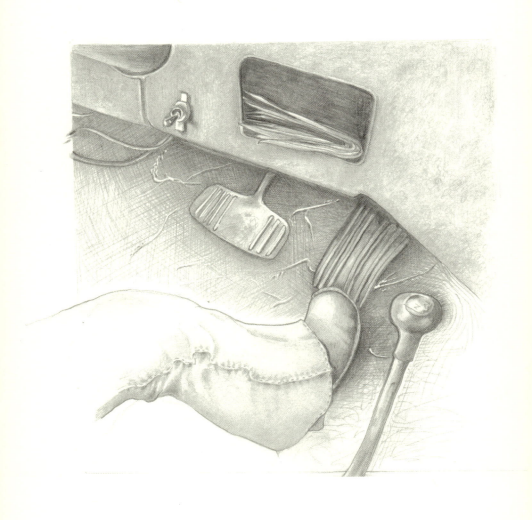

2

Funny Stories, Wandering Thoughts, and Laments

2008
Riding Horses in the Sandveld of South Africa

January

Picketburg, South Africa. Our cottage was in the middle of nowhere, in the desert, in what is known in Afrikaans as the Sandveld (dry sandy landscape). We were the only guests. I had told Jeanne there would be a swimming pool, and when we drove up and saw that it was no bigger than our dining room table, I exclaimed, "Well, it looked much bigger on their website." I further explained that they must have put a Barbie doll in the pool floating on a raft to make the place look so luxurious.

After several hours, the caretaker-farmer came by to see how we were doing. He drove up in a small, dusty old pickup truck. He was white and barefoot, with long hair. His skin was leathery brown from working in the sun. There were two horses nearby, and Jeanne asked if we could ride them. After quizzing us about our riding skills, he said if we could catch them we could ride all we wanted. The small swimming pool and meager accommodations soon became irrelevant.

Jeanne sorted out the tack, and soon we were riding in the Sandveld of South Africa. I named my horse Zulu. It was so magical, with steep, rock-covered mountains in several directions and vast open desert in others. The weather was perfect, the air was clear, and there wasn't another human anywhere in sight. We were alone, on horseback in Africa—one of those romantic moments that will never be forgotten.

Reflections on South Africa

An oppressed majority will eventually take over. Democracy does not necessarily lead to less violence or poverty.

2011
Rockets in Swoope

The Valley Rocket Club resubmitted its request to launch fourteen-foot rockets in Swoope. How is it that some outsiders, not owning any land here, can come in and launch rockets in a farming community against the wishes of all the adjoining landowners? The rocketeers are slick and polished, with a website for the world to see. They have lots of outsider influence helping them push their agenda down the throats of the locals.

During the public hearing on the matter, the rocket folks stated that launching rockets in Swoope would promote agritourism. One neighbor, Betty Jo Hamilton, spoke against the special use permit to allow rocket launches. She brought a two-foot-long rocket with her that she found in one of her farming fields six miles from the launch site. She disagreed with their argument and said, "When my cows launch rockets, that will be agritourism!"

What's up with all this?

You find a love, a place, and then along comes a carpetbagger . . . the rocket club . . . adults really, wanting to play games with their fourteen-foot missiles, infringing on the rights of others with their shocking noises and potential threats of fires and trespass; all farmers in the area live in fear of their barns burning down. The rocketeers don't even live here. It's no different than a cruise ship coming to harbor in the Galapagos or Montego Bay or Road Town, British Virgin Islands.

Years ago, the city of Staunton annexed the farms in the adjacent county. This was against the wishes of the landowners, who just wanted to keep farming. The city immediately rezoned the farmers' properties from agriculture to various urban uses and told them their taxes would be raised accordingly. The city justified these hostile takings because they needed more revenue.

The Takings
Cruise ships and tourists invade the Galapagos
City Council claims farmland for tax revenue
Rocketeers invade the pastures of Swoope
Multinationals frack the Appalachians for natural gas
BP goes deep for oil
It's all invasive, outsiders taking what's not theirs
Nazis taking over Poland
Europeans taking over North America
Is it any different?

2016
Drought in Kruger National Park

Anna is our Mother Teresa. Sometimes I feel that she is more family to Jeanne than her own mother. Both cried today when Anna told Jeanne she was going to give her a used table cloth.

We are tourists in a war zone. South Africa lost nine hundred rhinos to poachers last year. Rangers have killed 168 poachers and three hundred have been arrested.

Emotions: Helplessness and sorrow for the animals that have to endure this drought and heat. Encouraged by Anna's strength.

Amazed at Janni's knowledge of the natural world. Endeared to the woman I love ... Jeanne. She loves it here. She loves the animals, especially the Giraffes and Elephants. She is coming around to the birds. She loved the Black Crake with its babies today.

Poor Janni and Hannelie. They have a Down syndrome baby who must have open-heart surgery.

Chris, Anna's best friend, uses a wheelchair. She joined us tonight at the dinner table, and though she could hardly talk, she enjoyed the slideshow of the pictures we took in Kruger National Park.

Kruger National Park is suffering the worst drought in perhaps a century. It's doubly bad because this is the "rainy season," and yet there is no rain. In several weeks, the dry season begins, when nothing grows much. The Lowveld (low elevation field) during this rainy season is essentially a desert. No grass whatsoever. Windblown swirls of detached soil particles rise up and dance across the veld. I can see three, four, five of them in the distance. The only vegetation is the remaining leaves on scrubby shrubs and stunted trees. We see Impala, Kudu, Waterbuck, Giraffes, and Elephants picking leaves off the trees and Warthogs on their knees, eating the remaining stubs of dead grass and then pulling the plants up by their roots to feed.

As we drove toward Skukuza Camp, we saw rain falling from dark clouds in the distance. We could smell the rain. Oh, what a beautiful sight and smell. Fortunately, we drove right into it. We stopped to feel it and hear it soaking into the parched earth. I have heard it many times on our farm in Virginia when the land is parched. If you stop and listen you can hear it. The water goes straight into every dry crevice in the earth. As the water soaks in, I can hear the air being expelled. It is a soft gurgling. The earth is drinking, saying AAAAHHHHhhhhhh. To stop and listen to the sound of the land drinking is soothing to my soul. The animals were jubilant. The plants, on the edge of death began growing. The gears of life's cycles, at a standstill for lack of lubrication, began to move.

> **JEANNE'S LINK TO SOUTH AFRICA** *Jeanne's father, Cornelius "Neil" Hoffman was born and raised in South Africa. Anna is Neil's first cousin and owns a farm near Kruger National Park. Janni is Anna's nephew and is married to Hannelie.*

2003
Why I Eat What I Do

What we eat reflects how we live. The American fast-paced, give it to me, chug it down, precooked, processed, refined, preserved, prepackaged product (so I can get the kid to soccer practice) supports the same kind of agriculture.

What I choose to eat does not have anything to do with spirituality. I want to eat food that is produced in a manner that supports the careful use of our natural resources, and I want to support the local farmer who does that.

2004
Loggerhead Shrike Sighting

For the first time in three years I saw a Loggerhead Shrike on North Mountain Road in Swoope.

The smallest songbird of prey in America, this once common species is in steep decline. Its population plummeted seventy-six percent between 1966 and 2015 according to the North American Breeding Bird Survey. There are less than one hundred left in Virginia and no known breeding pairs in Augusta County. We may have had the last breeding pair of this magnificent bird on the farm.

The name Loggerhead Shrike (*Lanius ludovicianus*) is revealing. Its genus name, *Lanius,* is Latin for butcher, and shrike is a derivative of shriek. The bird doesn't really have a pretty song; rather, it shrieks.

It also has a dark mask over its eyes . . . a shrieking butcher with a mask; very appropriate for this robin-size bird. Its diet consists of small birds, large insects, and mice, which it usually kills with a blow to the back of the neck with its beak, stunning them. The bird impales the stunned prey on a thorn and uses its small raptor-like beak to tear the animal's flesh.

Once abundant from Canada to Central America, shrikes have essentially disappeared from the northeastern part of the U.S. Virginia lists the bird as "endangered" because there have been only two to ten sightings of breeding pairs in recent years.

Shrikes are in Swoope because of ideal habitat: vast acreage of grassland with scattered trees and shrubs, many, such as the Hawthorn, with thorns. This is cattle country, so the birds can also use barbed-wire fences to impale their prey.

It's still a mystery why their population is declining; ample habitat exists, especially here in the Shenandoah Valley of Virginia.

2008
Basket Case

I rode home from work and saw some orange flagging on many trees. I asked around and no one seemed to know what was going on. Jeanne knew the head of the VDOT maintenance shop, so she gave him a call. He told her they were marking the trees to be taken down because they were a hazard to motorists.

After she got off the phone with him, I asked her whether they knew we were in a Loggerhead Shrike sighting zone, and she said she doubted they knew that such a creature existed.

It just so happened that I was the contracting officer for USDA programs that awards contracts for land and water stewardship practices, one of which is the protection of endangered species habitat.

Two contracts in the Middlebrook area for the Grassland Reserve Program were awarded extra qualifying points because the farms were within two miles of a sighting of the Loggerhead Shrike.

I've seen the birds and have logged sightings myself with the agency that is the repository for the information, the Virginia Department of Conservation and Recreation's Division of Natural Heritage.

From my USDA office the next morning, I called the VDOT office in charge of putting the orange flagging on the trees. I told them that I was the district conservationist and was inquiring about the flagging along the roads in Swoope.

I asked to speak to the manager on duty. He said they marked the trees to be cut down because if they fell over on a car, VDOT could be liable for the damages.

I asked him whether he knew the trees were in an endangered species habitat area for the Loggerhead Shrike.

He replied, "Oh, we know all about the Longaberger Shrike."

I said, "This isn't about a basket; it's about a bird. I'd like to talk to your supervisor."

They ended up not felling the trees.

2013
Jeanne Wouldn't Hire Me

Jeanne's shoulder is recovering nicely. She had surgery three weeks ago. Dr. Otteni did it arthroscopically. Now, while her shoulder is recovering, I must do the feeding of the cows with the hydra-bed truck while she gets the gates. The first time she wanted to go with me to feed I said, "You can go, but no bitchin'!" I was sure she would let me know, in every detail, what I was doing wrong. I was right, and she started immediately.

"Get your foot off the clutch," she yelled. "Why are you going that way?" she asked. The litany of instructions and questions continued.

This went on for days, and we each were extremely tolerant of the other. One day I said, "You know, I would not work for you."

"Well, I wouldn't hire you," she replied immediately.

"Well, I wouldn't apply for the job" I said.

"Well, I wouldn't give you an application," she replied.

2015
Persian Wool in the Hot Tub: Romance in Luray

Luray, Virginia. Last night was so much fun. We are in Luray staying at the Mimslyn Inn. Cocktails at six, dinner and a show at seven. It was a Valentine celebration.

During the cocktail hour, a winter storm began. It was very cold, way below freezing; the wind howled and snow swirled all around. People came in from the front parking lot totally covered in snow. The average age of the group must have been seventy. Visibility was less than ten feet.

The inn had a live band and a guy singing Frank Sinatra songs. Jeanne usually doesn't like to dance, but this evening she wanted to dance practically every dance. We brought our own wine, a Moulderbosh Faithful Hound Cabernet. Jeanne got the server to bring us real red wine glasses.

After the show, lots of dancing, and a great dinner, we went upstairs to our room. Jeanne looked out our second-story room window and saw the hot tub.

"Look honey, there's a hot tub. Let's get in," she said.

"You are kidding," I replied.

She was determined. We both stripped down and put our winter coats on. Jeanne, totally naked underneath her black Persian lamb full length coat . . . . Wow, she looked so beautiful.

We walked out the back door onto the snow-covered sidewalk. The gate to the hot tub was locked. Jeanne walked back in to the

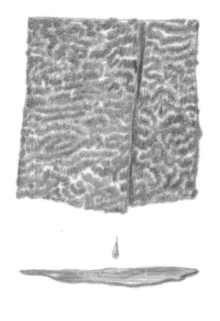

front desk to ask if someone could unlock it.

While Jeanne was gone, I noticed the gate was locked with a bike lock with ample length to squeeze through, which I did.

Jeanne came back and informed me that they couldn't open it because it was after nine.

We both squeezed through the gate. Jeanne walked up to the edge of the hot tub. I couldn't wait to see her disrobe.

To my total amazement she took one step in and her whole body, full-length coat and all, totally submerged. Blllooooop, down she went. My jaw dropped to the frozen sidewalk. I thought the weight of the wet coat would drown her.

I disrobed, raced to the edge and grabbed her by the collar of the coat to pull her up. Thank God, the water was warm. She slithered out of the coat, and there I was, stark naked holding the thirty pounds of dripping wet coat in twenty-degree weather.

"Come on, get in," Jeanne said.

I draped the coat over a chair and got in. We swam for a few minutes, and then we heard a siren. . . . Oh my, had they called the cops on us?

We both got out, grabbed a towel, and I put my coat on Jeanne. I grabbed the wet full-length curly lamb coat, now frozen and somewhat stiff and managed to squeeze through the locked gate. Thank goodness, the back door did not lock on us.

Upstairs in our room, I hung the wet coat in the shower while Jeanne lamented about the death of her Persian wool coat.

Next morning, we sobered up, and a thought hit me, "Oh my God, I wonder if they had a surveillance camera on us?"

I took my coffee out to the pool to look around, and damn, sure enough, they had one pointing right at the hot tub.

When we were checking out, Jeanne asked whether anyone had turned in her red wine purse, and the clerk, possibly recognizing us, said, "Yes, and how about this pearl bracelet?" Sure enough, they both belonged to Jeanne.

"Some people just have too much fun," the clerk said, looking straight into Jeanne's eyes.

I will be sixty years old this year . . . and having this much fun? Jeanne is so much fun to be with.

2016
Leap Day for the Chesapeake Bay Watershed

February 29, the Supreme Court of the United States refuses to hear the *American Farm Bureau Federation v. Environmental Protection Agency* case. The ruling of the Third Circuit Court of Appeals stands.

Five years of court battles are over. The day after the U.S. EPA accepted all six of the Chesapeake Bay state's plans, collectively known as the Chesapeake Clean Water Blueprint, to meet pollution reduction targets, the American Farm Bureau Federation and other deep-pocketed organizations with polluting interests, such as the Fertilizer Institute and the American Home Builders Association, sued the EPA.

They claimed the EPA used flawed science to establish pollution reduction targets. They claimed the EPA overstepped its bounds, and they claimed the EPA failed to give people enough time to comment on the blueprint.

On September 13, 2013, Federal District Court Judge Sylvia Rambo ruled in favor of the EPA. Her ninety-eight-page ruling confirmed that the EPA acted within its Clean Water Act authority. She added that the EPA's role was critical for the complex multistate watershed cleanup.

The polluters appealed her decision. They lost again before a Third Circuit Court of Appeals panel of three judges. They appealed to the U.S. Supreme Court.

Sadly, oddly, strangely, Supreme Court Justice Antonin Scalia, a very conservative member of the court died leaving the court with four justices on the left and four on the right. This no doubt had something to do with the court's decision to not hear the case. This meant that the lower court's decision stands and becomes the law of the land in the Third Circuit.

2017
My Daughter Lives on Top of Houston Black Soil

My daughter, Heather, and her husband, Shane, live in Forney, Texas. Their house is in a new subdivision carved out of the Blackland Prairie, part of the Great Plains. As we walked their dog this morning, I could not help but be amazed at how black the soil is. I stopped and dug up a piece with my knife. I put some in my hand and smelled it. Smells rich. I spit on it and it made a long ribbon when I smushed it with my fingers. I checked the soil survey app on my phone and learned it was the state soil of Texas, "Houston Black." It has a high clay content with very high shrink-swell characteristics. I'm surprised there is so much development on this soil. Foundations will crack because when the soil is wet, it expands, when the soil is dry it shrinks.

"Maybe there is some engineering breakthrough," I thought.

After some research, I found out that the developer installed an irrigation system around the foundation of the houses to keep the soil at a constant moisture content. Heather and Shane have to pay the water bill to do that, and the system is mandatory according to the homeowner's association.

Of Pelicans, Pterodactyls, and Petroleum

Hagerman National Wildlife Refuge (NWR), Texas. Colossal oil rig contraptions—they remind me of pterodactyls—giant, winged, reptiles that roamed the earth millions of years ago. These reptiles became extinct with all the other dinosaurs in the late Cretaceous Period some seventy million years ago. Their bodies formed the massive crude oil deposits we now extract.

Hagerman NWR is home to much wildlife and the oil rigs that churn up the crude oil made from the decomposed dinosaurs.

Breathing in the irony of the moment: These oil rig pterodactyls will become extinct in my daughter's lifetime, hopefully extinguishing the carbon dioxide emissions from burning all this Cretaceous crude.

On one of the islands in the refuge we broke out a picnic of sandwiches, veggies, and sauvignon blanc.

It was a moment...

The oil rigs churning, a breeze, wide open expanses of wetlands and water.... Overhead, a flock of big white birds with huge heads descended slowly without any motion, floating down onto a small spit of land three hundred yards in the distance. White Pelicans. They sort of look like pterodactyls.

2006
Hemlocks and Aphids

March

We hiked up Ramsey's Draft, a wilderness area of the George Washington National Forest. There, we saw the poor, ancient hemlocks succumbing to the Wooly Adelgid Aphid, a tiny soft-bodied insect with a piercing sucking mouthpart that truly sucks the life out of the tree's needles. The extinction of a species is happening right before our eyes, and it is so lamentable.

Five Acres in the Country

I now sit in the living room of Meadowview. A fire is chasing the chilled dampness from the room. I can hear a Robin singing, along with an occasional cow calmly talking to her calf. Sparse raindrops falling on the tin roof and the crackling of the fire provide great ambiance to this calming moment.

People who are fortunate enough to own land should understand that what they do with their land profoundly affects the water quality of everyone downstream.

I gnash my teeth at the people who buy a five-acre tract in the country that once was part of a real farm that supported myriad wildlife. The fencerows, odd areas, and weedy patches disappear under the blade of the bulldozer. Homeowners spend a significant amount of their life mowing their sterile five-acre lawn. These people come into my office and ask me what they can do to attract more wildlife. I'm sure I must have a dumb look on my face.

History has clearly shown that all cultural and political collapses are rooted in the lack of environmental stewardship.

Loggerhead Shrikes and 'No' to Habitat

My mother-in-law is a self-proclaimed "birder." She understands that Loggerhead Shrikes are very rare; in fact, they are considered extremely rare and critically imperiled in the Commonwealth of Virginia. We have a nesting pair in the hedgerow in the pasture behind the house.

The fence was in need of repair but those repairs would destroy the habitat where we have seen the shrikes.

It would be vital to plant shrike habitat along with replacing the fence. I had a conversation with Jeanne's mother trying to convince her to replace the habitat.

I asked her if it would be okay for me to plant a few trees in the hedgerow where the shrike nested last year.

"What did you have in mind?" she asked.

"Would a Hawthorn be okay?"

"Oh no, they spread," she replied.

"Well, how about a mulberry?"

"Oh no, they are too messy."

"How about a Tulip Poplar?"

"Oh no, they are too weak."

"How about a Dogwood?"

"No."

"Ash?"

"No."

"Oak?"

"No."
"Maple?"
"No."
"Well, what kind of tree would you like?"
"Well, none at all!"

2008
Loggerhead Shrike Sighting

Today we saw a pair of Loggerhead Shrikes in the Wheatlands hedgerow.

2012
Loggerhead Shrike Sighting

Saw two Loggerhead Shrikes on Cattleman Road between Croft's pond and Godfrey's place.

2013
Shoulder Therapy

Jeanne is going to therapy for her shoulder, and she is not supposed to lift anything with her left arm. Today she was carrying an armload of wood with her left arm.

"You're not supposed to lift anything with that arm," I scolded.

"I'm not lifting, I'm carrying. They didn't say I couldn't carry," she replied.

2014
Annie Oakley and the Groundhog in the Culvert

This afternoon Jeanne and I were coming back from the Wheatlands field and turning into the driveway when we spotted a groundhog. It ran into the culvert in our driveway.

"Get Dexter and the gun!" Jeanne shouted. Dexter is our trusty Border Collie who is always eager to kill a groundhog.

Bob, our part-time helper on the farm during calving season, was waiting in the driveway for us. This was going to be good. Jeanne instructed us to watch the ends of the culvert so that the hog could not escape. She went in the house for the pistol and Dexter.

It was immediately comical, and as I stood at one end of the culvert and Bob at the other, I said to the hog in the culvert, "You're surrounded. Come out with your hands up."

Jeanne came out with the gun and handed it to me. She crawled down to the west end of the culvert and asked me to hand her the gun. I did.

"Is it cocked and loaded?" she asked.

I said, "It's loaded, pull the hammer back and it's ready."

I covered Dexter's ears. She was on her belly looking into the culvert, and she shot a round. A 22-caliber hollow-point shot into an 18-inch culvert sounds like a cannon going off.

Seven shots later . . . the hog had apparently been killed by Jeanne, a.k.a. Annie Oakley. Bob said, "If it isn't dead, it's deaf. Probably get run over by a car."

2007
Earth Day and the American Bittern

... much later, maybe around 7 p.m., during the Earth Day party at Meadowview, I took several interested people to see our special visitor. We walked quietly to the wet area below the pond, and lo and behold, there it was in full view where everyone could see it. How could one not be moved by seeing such a strange bird? We were so lucky, the American Bittern is a long-distance migrator, on its way to Canada to breed. There are only a few recorded sightings of this bird in Augusta County.

I Am So Lucky

I walk around the yard looking at all the buds and flowers. It's amazing. I am so fortunate. I live on a farm. I actually live on a farm. I feel so lucky. And even with all the conflict between generations and hard work and endless chores, the fulfillment far outweighs the trifling amount of baggage. I can plant trees, grow our own food, care for livestock, be outside every day—yes, even when I'm in the cold with numb fingers, I love it. I especially like sharing this with the woman I love.

2008
Shenandoah Oak Stakes Outsourced to Iowa

I was a lowly bureaucrat in 2008 working for the USDA Natural Resources Conservation Service. George W. Bush was president on a mission to outsource government jobs to the private sector.

That year, the government "outsourced" my ability to obtain wooden surveyors' stakes that I use to mark off conservation areas. A private company from Cedar Rapids, Iowa, won the bid to provide us with stakes. The freight alone to ship their stakes, made from cedar, to the Shenandoah Valley cost more than the oak stakes I usually purchased from a local saw mill.

I used the cedar stakes several months ago to delineate a twenty-five-acre conservation area. Fence builders use my stakes to drive their corner posts for the fences that will keep livestock out of streams.

I got a call from one of my clients. She said the fence builder was on site, but all my stakes were gone. It didn't take me long to figure out that the cattle had destroyed all but two of the fifty-five stakes it took to mark the job off. Cedar wood is soft and brittle. A mature cow on average weighs a thousand pounds. When cows scratch their heads on the stake, it will easily break off.

After much consternation, I received "an exception" from a purchasing officer to once again buy stakes locally, and I got some good old oak stakes from a local sawmill that would not break upon the influence of cattle. I have been in public service for twenty-nine years, and I don't have any good data to support "outsourcing." In this case it cost the taxpayers triple: waste in freight, waste in an inferior product, and a waste of my time, because I had to lay this job off twice.

So when politicians claim they cut government spending and government jobs and claim the private sector can do it more efficiently, dig a little deeper, follow the money, and I'll bet it's not true.

2010
Roll-Start the Truck? It Did Not Work!

Jeanne called me at work to inform me that the hydra-bed truck (just back from the shop) would not start. She wanted me to come home early so I could help her roll-start it. Her mother, Jean, and I arrived at about the same time. Jeanne decided that because her mother was there, we would use her Dodge Durango to pull the hydra-bed truck. I got in my mother-in-law's car, and Jeanne hooked up the chain. Jeanne got into the hydra-bed and gave me the signal to drive forward. It would be an easy pull.

I started slowly and once I was rolling, I could feel Jeanne popping the clutch in the truck to make it start. Nothing happened for maybe four attempts. Then I could hear Jeanne cursing. I looked back, and she was giving me some "kung fu" type gestures with her arms. We stopped, and Jeanne got out, fuming and cursing. She quickly walked up to my window and said I needed to drive faster.

So we tried again and again, each time faster, and each time she popped the clutch I could visualize the guts of my mother-in-law's car being yanked out onto the road. This went on for a half a mile, all the way up to Cattleman Road. We turned around and started back. Pulling and yanking, pulling and yanking. This could not be good for Jean's car or for the son-in-law. I had had enough. I stopped and asked Jeanne to switch with me. As I got in the truck, I could not hear any sound from the fuel pump, so I raised the hood and saw the problem: the cable from the battery to the armature had melted in two.

Roll-starting this truck would never have worked. We had to get a new cable.

2013
Easter Letter to Family

Dear loved ones,

Happy Easter. We are truly blessed to have you as family and friends. We hope this communication finds you healthy and happy. We miss you very much and hope to see you soon. Please know that you are welcome at Meadowview anytime.

Jeanne and I are both very happy and are enjoying a roaring fire in the fireplace on this Easter Sunday between feeding the cows and tending to newborns—three so far today.

We have had some peculiar weather here in Swoope the last couple of weeks. And although it appears beautiful, it has been a tremendous ordeal for us while our cows are bringing new babies into the world.

The past few weeks have been the peak of calving, during the worst possible weather—wet and cold. On the worst day, March 27, eight calves were born and one perished. Jeanne's knowledge of cattle, their behavior and needs, and her attention to detail saved at least five newborns. There was one forty-eight-hour period from March 26 through 28 that was a marathon for us: we slept little, got covered in mud and afterbirth, became exhausted, cried, cursed, laughed, and held each other in moments of both grief and joy.

The land was saturated with water, leaving not a dry spot on the farm. A cow giving birth on land this wet, with temperatures right at freezing, faces the ingredients for death. We were all over it. A cattleman's "moment" if you will. Jeanne was ever vigilant. Luckily, we were both "not working" our regular jobs and available to respond to the unfolding events of a harsh spring combined with a full moon and scores of pregnant cows.

We ended up putting two nearly frozen calves in the calf cooker, which restored their lives, bringing one in the house for the night and bottle-feeding two in the field.

I "tubed" my first calf and received a promotion from "gate boy" to "tuber"—not the potato. It may sound funny, but it's a very important job. The act of tubing is done when a newborn is so cold or weak that it cannot suck its mother's teat, a nipple on a bottle, or even your finger. We have a special feeding tube with a little ball on the end of it that is inserted very carefully down the esophagus of the calf and into the rumen. Once in the rumen, colostrum is poured via a funnel into the tube and into the rumen. It gives the baby the nourishment needed to stay alive.

During all this bad weather and calving we only lost one calf, and we both blame ourselves for it. If we had only been more vigilant. If we had only been stronger.

I think a lot of people don't realize how dedicated farmers are to their livestock. Jeanne cares for each cow—120 of them—and for each of their babies, as if they were her own children. And if we lose a single one, to exposure, coyotes, vultures, or through lack of attention or endurance or some other aberration, she feels it's her fault. Jeanne is truly a great herdswoman, and I admire her faithful care for the animals, her tireless bravery through adverse conditions, and her determination to succeed.

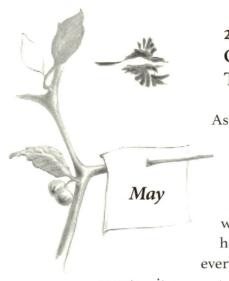

2009
One Acre Every Ten Seconds

As a society, we are losing our best farmland at a pace that is unsustainable. To those of us at the local level, it doesn't seem to affect us too much when we lose a hundred acres here or there. But added up, from every small community across the country, it amounts to a whopping 3,236,643 acres a year (U.S. Census of Agriculture 2007). That's one acre lost every ten seconds.

We have something even more special here in the Valley; our farmland can support rain-fed agriculture. In other words, our food production here does not depend on irrigation water from deep wells or dams. There aren't very many places like that in the world.

2010
The Disconnect Between the Land and Food

When I was kid everybody I knew had been in a barn and fed animals of some kind. I fed pigs and chickens and cows on Mr. Larsen's farm. He had one of those 1930s farms with a little bit of everything. He even had a workhorse named Bob. He milked cows by hand and kept the milk in those metal containers in the springhouse. The cold water from the spring cooled the milk. People buy those antique metal milk containers now and put flowers in them. He had a huge vegetable garden and made deliveries all over the neighborhood.

My sister boarded her horse at his farm, and we would often play in the hayloft. After school, I would walk to Mr. Larsen's farm and help him with chores such as gathering eggs from the hens in the chicken coop or slopping the hogs.

We have had many families visit us here at Meadowview, and I am amazed at how many children have never been in a barn or know what a bale of hay is. They seem to enjoy it when we show them even the most elementary things about farm life. The current disconnects people have between the land and the soil, where their food comes from, and the table where they eat is as wide as the Grand Canyon and it is getting wider. How can people love the land without feeling it? We must do more.

2011
Bobby's in the Hoffman Farm Rodeo

We used the horses to move the cows that were still pregnant and the bulls into the field closer to the barn. Once that task was completed, Jeanne wanted to ride up over the hill to check the amount of mineral in the feeder. The horses were feeling good. As we crossed a small swale, Oakey, my horse, broke into full bucking. I began pulling on one rein as I had been taught.

Jeanne immediately yelled, "SIT UP!"

I managed to sit up a little, but it's hard to do when your horse is trying to buck you off. I dropped one rein and was using both hands to pull the left rein in, all the while the bucking continued.

Jeanne yelled, "RAISE YOUR HAND!" "RAISE YOUR HAND!"

I thought, "What? Raise my hand?"

My God, I was pulling with both hands; how could I release one? The bucking continued and to my utter disbelief I was still in the saddle.

"RAISE YOUR HAND!" Jeanne shouted.

Okay, I thought, here goes . . .

I released my right hand and raised it high in the air; it flailed wildly as the bucking continued. Now I was in the rodeo.

I heard Jeanne say, "Oh my God." But it wasn't the kind of "Oh my God" of fear, it was more like an "Oh my God, I can't believe you did that."

She meant for me to raise the hand with the rein in it, thus pulling Oakey's head up. A horse can't buck with its head up.

Nonetheless, after a few more bucks he ceased his wild behavior. Jeanne was laughing her head off.

2013
This Is Where My Mother Is—Somewhere in the Never

I spent the morning birding. I started around Swoope and ended up at Sherando. The surprise birds today were the Willow Flycatchers at Wheatlands. I also saw a mink there in the wildlife area along the stream created through the Conservation Reserve Enhancement Program (CREP). CREP areas, regardless of how many trees have survived, are still magnificent habitats for all kinds of wildlife.

I was alone this morning, as I always am on Mother's Day. I go in search of her. I walk and think of old times and other lives. I go in search of answers; for what I don't know. Maybe something will come. Maybe I will think of a great metaphor or the truth of life.

This is where mom is now . . . somewhere in the never. I never see her, but I know she is here somewhere.

2016

This Mother's Day I took a bird hike and drove around, as I do most Mother's Days. Lots of treasure.

    Two bear cubs . . . and the mother
    Three American Chestnut stump sprouts
    Willow Flycatchers have arrived
    Lots of Worm-Eating Warblers on Little North Mountain
    Heard lots of Hooded Warblers

Thoughts of Mom: She was the Rachel Carson of my youth. As a child, she bought me a microscope and lab coat. I formed a science club. It was such a wonder to look into a drop of water and see living things.

So now when I find treasure in nature, I find my mother as well.

2017

Yoga Retreat in Swoope and Bird Geeks

Vince Blackwood met me this morning at 7:30 to go birding. It was fifty-nine degrees and cloudy. Perfect for birding. Our first stop was the north bridge on Trimbles Mill Road. Middle River was only slightly brown, flowing full. Common Yellowthroats and Yellow Warblers greeted us immediately.

Orchard Oriole, Baltimore Oriole, Warbling Vireo.

Next, we drove into the north tributary crossing, parked, and walked to the river. Red-Headed Woodpecker, Willow Flycatchers.

Along the lower edge of the grazed woodland, I heard a Black-Throated Blue Warbler. Wow, what a bird. We actually saw it too.

Next, to the middle grazing pod. There I heard a call I had not heard in years, and I did not know what it was. I kept listening and watching. . . . Finally, it appeared: a Yellow-Breasted Chat! I had never seen one in Swoope.

We drove on Little North Mountain Road for a while, birding by ear. The roads are narrow here in Swoope; when two cars pass, each one must put a wheel off the road. When you are birding, you drive slowly and listen, stopping to see a singing bird.

A slow-moving car approached. The lady was driving as slowly as we were, so I thought she might be birding as well. I waved to the lady driver and she stopped.

"Is this a private road?" she asked. I don't think she had ever been on a public road this narrow.

"No ma'am, this is a public road," I replied.

"I'm going to a yoga retreat at the Four Winds. Am I on the right road?"

Four Winds is a horse ranch in Swoope that hosts trail rides and wedding events. It's pretty cool, with a bunkhouse, a bar, and lots of horses.

"Yes, it's just down the road on the right."

"How did you know to stop me?" she asked.

"Well, we're kinda geeky; we're birders," I said as I lifted my binos for her to see. "We thought you might be a birder."

"Well, I know all about geeky. My husband is a fruit fly biologist."

"Wow, that's really geeky," I replied in a slow, calm way.

Vince said, "My wife worked for the Smithsonian, illustrating fruit fly genitalia."

We all kind of looked at each other with kind smiles, knowing this was a pretty funny moment, but no one laughed.

She thanked us for directions and we continued our birding adventure.

In reflection, I think this is going to be one of the funniest stories of the year.

2005
Loggerhead Shrike Sighting

June

In the hedgerow behind the house we saw a pair of Loggerhead Shrikes, and then we saw one more.

2009
Successful Capitalists Must First Be Humanitarians

It is my observation that people who work for the sole purpose of making money are seldom happy. I know a few rich people who made a lot of money off people's ignorance or poor choices, and they seem miserable. Successful entrepreneurs, in my opinion, provide a service or make a product contributing to the well-being of mankind as a priority. Money is secondary. People are content or fulfilled when their efforts help people. Therefore, a successful capitalist must first be a humanitarian.

2012
Country Dog Dexter in the Big City

River Towers Condominium, Wilmington, Delaware. Jeanne and I were taking Dexter for a walk without a leash. A couple came out of the condominium complex with their little obnoxious city dog on one of those retractable leashes that will let a dog out maybe twenty-five feet. As soon as Jeanne saw the little dog, she laid Dexter down and knelt beside him. She knew Dexter would want to take the little morsel out. Dexter doesn't do well with other dogs, especially little city dogs. The man holding the leash let his dog out, way out, and the dog ran right over to me and began smelling me and jumping up on my legs. I wanted to kick the dog but kept my composure. The owner did nothing. He just let him jump all over me. It was ridiculous. I think he thought I would enjoy his precious little brat dog. Then he let his dog smell Dexter. Oh boy, that man was pushing Jeanne's button—and Dexter's. I thought things were going to deteriorate rapidly. Every muscle in Dexter's body was tense, and he was drooling.

"You're asking for trouble," Jeanne said to the man. I know Jeanne, and my interpretation of that was, "Your little f___ dog is fixin' to die, mister!"

"You're asking for trouble," she repeated. He finally reeled his damn dog in and went on his way. Jeanne did really a good job of holding her composure.

2014
The Princess of Swoope Goes to Washington to See the President

Jeanne, the Princess of Swoope, and I had the privilege of attending the League of Conservation Voters annual Capital Dinner on June 25. It was held in the Ronald Reagan Building and International Trade Center in the nation's capital. We were invited because I am on the board of the Virginia League of Conservation Voters. President Barack Obama and Senator Tim Kane were keynote speakers.

Over eight hundred people attended, all dressed for an evening of inspiration and fun. Jeanne wore her "princess" outfit. It has a turquoise, high-collar blouse and silky black pants. She wore a necklace with a big golden starfish on it and when she went through the two security check points it set off the alarms both times, prompting secret service agents to swarm around her with their metal detectors—part of the magic of the evening.

There was a walkway with green (as opposed to red) carpet and a wall of logos for picture taking. I was looking for the fashion police but didn't see them. They would have had a field day with us because we were the only people not in black and white.

Once we got through the two security checkpoints and registration, we headed for the room where the president would speak. Our friend Roy Hoagland joined us, and we secured a spot directly behind the red rope. It was like being on the fifty-yard line in row A at a football game. Roy went to get us drinks from the open bar. There we were in front of the podium with the presidential seal and a huge American flag behind it. We knew then it was really going to happen.

By the time the speeches began, the place was packed and we were standing shoulder to shoulder with the movers and shakers of the conservation world.

It was a magical night filled with some of the most influential environmental people in the world. The many reporters there chose to focus on President Obama's lighthearted jabs at the science and climate change deniers instead of the success of what's going on in the real world or Jeanne's outfit.

Here's the main jab that they chose to report, from POTUS 44's actual text:

> THE PRESIDENT: It's pretty rare that you encounter people who say that the problem of carbon pollution is not a problem. You've all—in most communities and work places, et cetera, when you talk to folks, they may not know how big a problem, they may not know exactly how it works, they may doubt that we can do something about it, but generally they don't just say, no, I don't believe anything scientists say. (Laughter.) Except where?
>
> AUDIENCE: Congress!
>
> THE PRESIDENT: In Congress. (Laughter.) In Congress. Folks will tell you climate change is a hoax or a fad or a plot. (Laughter.) It's a liberal plot. (Laughter.) And then most recently, because many who say that actually know better and they're just embarrassed, they duck the question. They say, hey, I'm not a scientist, which really translates into, I accept that manmade climate change is real, but if I say so out loud, I will be run out of town by a bunch of fringe elements that thinks climate science is a liberal plot so I'm going to just pretend like, I don't know, I can't read. (Applause.)

The president talked for twenty minutes about real environmental issues, about the science behind them, and about how America is moving forward to solve these issues. Most of the media left this out, so I'm bringing it to you here. Here are some excerpts of what he said:

> THE PRESIDENT: We know that burning fossil fuels releases carbon dioxide. We know that carbon

dioxide traps heat. We know that the levels of carbon dioxide are higher than they've been in 800,000 years. We know that the twenty warmest years on record for our planet all happened since 1990—and last month was the warmest May ever recorded. We know that communities across the country are struggling with longer wildfire seasons, more severe droughts, heavier rainfall, more frequent flooding. That's why, last month, hundreds of experts declared that climate change is no longer a distant threat—it has moved firmly into the present. Those are the facts. You can ignore the facts; you can't deny the facts.

Right now, America generates more clean energy than ever before. Thanks in part to the investments we made in the Recovery Act. (Applause) Remember that old Recovery Act? (Laughter) It was the largest investment in green energy and technology in U.S. history—that was just one of its attributes.

As a consequence of those investments, the electricity we generate from wind has tripled since 2008. (Applause) The energy we generate from the sun, has increased more than tenfold. (Applause) Every four minutes, another American home or business goes solar. And last year alone, solar jobs jumped 20 percent.

Since I took office, we've doubled how far our cars and trucks will go on a gallon of gas by the middle of the next decade.

Today, about 40 percent of America's carbon pollution comes from our power plants. There are no federal limits to the amount those plants can pump into the air. None. We limit the amount of toxic chemicals like mercury, and sulfur, and arsenic in our air and water, but power plants can dump as much carbon pollution into our atmosphere as they want. It's not smart, it's not right, it's not safe, and I am determined it needs to stop.

I should point out, by the way, that we're not just acting on climate change; we're also doing more for conservation. (Applause) Since I took office, we've established ten new national parks, ten new National Wildlife Refuges, eleven new national monuments. (Applause) I just announced plans to further protect our oceans.

https://obamawhitehouse.archives.gov/the-press-office/2014/06/25/remarks-president-league-conservation-voters-capital-dinner

2016
Richard's Package Gets Soaked

Jeanne's first day back at the U.S. Postal Service following surgery is interesting. She calls neighbor Richard to tell him he has three packages, and he says to put them on the porch beside the door. She says it is supposed to rain. He says, "That's okay just put them on the porch."

She gets home and wants to bush hog. After about twenty minutes a thunderstorm opens up. I pick her up.

"Oh my God, we've got to get Richard's packages!" she exclaims.

I take her to Richard's house in the car. I get out and race to the back of the car to get the umbrella. It's the kind of rain that even if you have an umbrella, you still get soaked. It was raining sideways, and I was soaked before I got to the umbrella.

We ran to the porch. There the cardboard packages were, in the corner. Unfortunately, the rain was more than his gutters would handle and in this particular corner the overflow of water amassed and overflowed onto the packages. It looked like Niagara Falls from Richard's roof.

The cardboard was so wet that it fell apart as we picked up the packages. We put them in the back of the car and called Richard to inform him of the predicament.

"No worries," he consoled us. "I'll come by your house to pick them up."

2015
A Special Spot

July

I've got a spot. The kind of spot that engages all your senses. I just want to sit and look at it. First, it engages my full spectrum of sight. Like being on the beach entranced by the ocean waves. My spot is on our front patio looking at all the flowers. The red impatiens draw my eyes in, then the white spires of the Black Cohosh, the light purple hostas . . . then the fireflies . . . Oh my, the sight.

Then the sounds . . . Robins and House Wrens. Many Robins settling in for the evening, chirping. There are so many of them that there is not a moment of silence.

It's damp from a day of drizzle and cool. Hard to believe that it is July and in the low sixties. It feels wonderful . . . just staring at the flowers.

2012
Global Warming Is Our DDT

August

This is the fiftieth anniversary of the publication of Rachel Carson's famous book *Silent Spring*. She must have felt helpless in a sea of corporate greed and public apathy because of the indiscriminate use of pesticides, especially DDT. We have Bald Eagles today because of her. That book also spawned the modern environmental movement, the passage of the Clean Water Act, the Clean Air Act, and the birth of the U.S. Environmental Protection Agency.

Today in her home county, Allegheny, Pennsylvania, a similar ecological disaster is unfolding: hydraulic fracturing, known as fracking, for natural gas. The same culprits are behind it: corporate greed and a wasteful American public duped by the propaganda of big energy.

What we call earth, corporations call "overburden": the soil and rocks that separate them from their "economic interest." True, our carbon dioxide emissions need to decrease, but at what cost? We can't know what fracking operations pump into our earth and our water because of proprietary rights, Halliburton greed, and a bought Congress. Odd, Rachel Carson, the champion that helped ban DDT was born in Allegheny County, the heart of fracking. I wish she were here to help us.

Global warming is the DDT of our time.

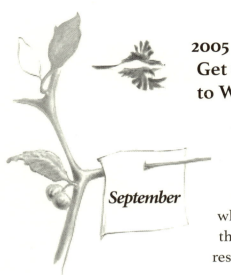

2005
Get Over It and Get to Work

Years ago, I quit trying to figure out why the administration needs the widgets they ask us for. I just dig in, give them what they think they need, and then get on with the real work of restoring the earth.

2007
Advice to New Employees

We are so fortunate in this country that we can still feed ourselves. Is this because our continent was settled last and we just haven't been here long enough to pillage our soil resources? Your job, hopefully fueled by your ethics, your passion to do something good for humankind, for the betterment of the earth, is to keep our topsoil out of our streams and improve it so generations to come can still feed themselves.

2009
Plastic Water Bottles: Symbol of Waste

To me one of the most infamous symbols of American arrogance, affluence, and grotesquely wasteful lifestyle is the plastic water bottle. While we slurp this water that is in most cases no better than tap water but costs more per gallon than gasoline, over a billion people will be searching for water in a hole in the ground and not have access to basic sanitation facilities—a billion! That is one-sixth of the world's population.

Empower Women

Stabilizing world population is the holy grail of sustainability, and empowering women is the most important strategy to achieve it.

2010
Forty Miles of Stream Exclusion and Champagne

We all drove down to Marvin Glover's farm after work and met with the fencing contractor Jack Clem. There I opened a bottle of champagne and passed around the bubbly to celebrate the fortieth mile of stream banks fenced off from cattle in a single year. It was our biggest year in history for a single field office.

2015
Joke Buddha and the Native Plant Society

I gave a humorous speech tonight to the Virginia Native Plant Society. The research began weeks ago. I wanted some humor, so I searched the internet for "native plant jokes." Joke Buddha was the first site that came up, and it stated that there were no native plant jokes.

I typed in "botany" and several jokes came up. The number-one joke on the internet for botany is this:

What did the stamen say to the stigma? I like your style.

This joke was greeted with roaring laughter. There was also a "dirty" joke that the program committee of the Virginia Native Plant Society would not let me tell.

Here it is:

So, there were these two squirrels sitting in a tree looking down on the forest floor. They saw a tree sapling, and one squirrel said to other, "Hey, that's a son-of-a birch."

"No, it isn't. It's a son-of-a beech," the other one said. Well, they argued for some time and after a while a woodpecker flew in and landed on the branch beside them. They asked the woodpecker if he would mind going down to investigate.

"Not at all," he replied.

So he swooped down to investigate. He returned, and the squirrels inquired, "Well, what was it, a son-of-a birch or a son-of-a beech?

The woodpecker replied, "Well, I don't know, but there was a hell of a nice piece of ash down there."

2006
'Mista Clicka'

October

I was the district conservationist in the Headwaters Soil and Water Conservation District in 2005, the year USDA selected the South Fork of the Shenandoah River watershed for its premier Conservation Security Program (CSP). It was America's first green payment program, awarding farmers who went above and beyond simply producing food. We gave payments for sequestering carbon, preserving wildlife habitat, protecting water quality, maintaining soil quality, and a whole host of other green activities.

It was a great program for rewarding stewardship, but it was very complicated. Our agency had just come into the real technological age of electronic signatures. I was used to going out in the field to certify an agricultural practice, signing a form with a real pen, and handing that paper to the clerk, who would process the payment.

That was real simple. But, hey, the computer is going to save us time and paper and money.

We had thirty-five CSP contracts in the Headwaters District in 2005. I started making stewardship payments for the programs using the new, efficient electronic signature. It took . . . me . . . forever . . . to . . . process . . . a . . . payment!

I counted the mouse clicks to make a single payment for the program. It took sixty-six.

I was so proud of myself for figuring out just how "efficient" this process was that I called the person in charge of the program to inform him.

"Do you know how many clicks it takes to make one payment for this program? Sixty-six," I said.

"Well, we are just going to call you Mista Clicka," he replied.

2007
Howard's RV, the Walmart Parking Lot, and Jeanne

Howard is an old friend of Jean and Jeanne's. He's probably in his late seventies. He lives in an RV and travels back and forth across the country between New York and California. He has done everything, has the T-shirt to prove it, and readily tells you all about it.

When he travels through Virginia, he calls both Jean and Jeanne to invite them to eat dinner with him. Almost every time they go, he forgets his wallet. This has happened so many times Jean and Jeanne try to avoid an encounter with him.

One time was unusual. Both Jeanne and Jean refused to have dinner with him, but upon his relentless insistence, Jeanne accepted his offer to have coffee with him in his RV, which was parked overnight in the Walmart parking lot in Staunton. The RV folks have their own Walmart parking lot culture, and Howard was a regular "parker."

Jeanne agreed to meet him for coffee before her shoulder therapy session. It was a warm day, so she decided to drive the Ford Thunderbird, retro convertible with the top down.

After their twenty-minute-or-so coffee visit, Howard followed her out of the RV to her parked convertible. There he hugged her good-bye and gave her a kiss on the cheek. Jeanne had no idea what that looked like to an admiring observer, and when she went to the nearby Burger King down the street, the admiring observer followed her in and tried repeatedly to strike up a conversation with her until it dawned on her that he thought she was a hooker.

2009
Mr. Hill Destroyed the Farm

And now after twenty years of errant soil erosion that is clearly evident, a new farmer will begin the process of healing this land. What took one thousand years to build, Mr. Hill destroyed in twenty. With thirty years of field experience I can honestly say that even though one cannot see sheet erosion, what they taught us in history about soil erosion and what they taught us in science about soil erosion prediction is true. Those who farm beyond the limits of sustainability eventually go out of business. Our current law allows farmers to plant crops in ways that allow soil erosion to occur at twice the level that our soil resources can withstand. The law that allows this, the U.S. Farm Bill, may be a good example of political compromise, but it is an example of reckless natural resource management.

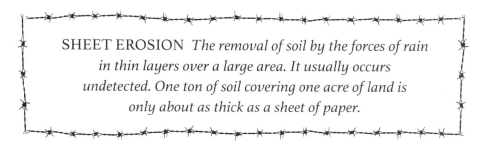

SHEET EROSION *The removal of soil by the forces of rain in thin layers over a large area. It usually occurs undetected. One ton of soil covering one acre of land is only about as thick as a sheet of paper.*

2011
Peak Fecal

White-Crowned Sparrows arrived today.

Yesterday I had a conversation with the director of our local water and sewer service authority. He stated that when he came here twenty-five years ago, he could find wells and springs that had no fecal coliform. He cannot find any today.

Just as we have reached "Peak Oil" and "Peak Water" in many parts of the world, we have now reached "Peak Fecal." And we are at the top of the watershed. No one else could have done this; we did it to ourselves.

Pay It Forward: No Tonic Water in Middlebrook Store

On my return to Meadowview from McKinley, I received a call from our friend Jeff Sampson (from Delaware) who was staying the weekend. He said he'd forgotten the only thing Jeanne had asked him to bring: tonic water. He asked if I was anywhere near a store.

I was just south of Middlebrook, population maybe fifty, and they had recently reopened the old general store. I told Jeff that I was indeed near a store and to not worry about the tonic water. I pulled into the parking spot at the store—they only have one—and walked in. There were two people in the store: a lady behind the cash register and a man about my age.

"Excuse me but do you happen to have any tonic water?" I asked.

They both looked at each other in a puzzled way, and the lady said, "I don't know. Let's go have a look."

The gentleman followed us and said to me a low voice, "It's kinda hard to make a gin and tonic without tonic water." We both laughed, and we all searched the two aisles in the store to no avail.

He asked me which way I was going, and I replied, "Toward Swoope," and gestured with my hand pointing to the west.

"Do you know where Haytie Lane is?" he asked.

"Oh yes, I'll go right past it on my way home," I replied.

"Well, why don't you follow me to my house. I have some tonic water that I will give you."

I followed him to the fourth driveway on the right, and there he gave me a six-pack of small tonic waters. He would not take any payment but asked me to "pay it forward," meaning to do something kind for someone down the road. What a grand place we live in.

2013
We Checked Every Mailbox

Last Saturday and Sunday Jeanne and I rode around her rural route in her new Jeep to check every mailbox for minimum height.

She hadn't slept in weeks. Her old red Jeep turned out to be a lemon, and it overheated frequently while she delivered mail. She would call me in great agitation, screaming into the phone about how she felt . . . using plenty of adjectives.

She finally broke down and bought a new right-hand-drive Jeep. I don't think she has ever bought a new vehicle. The poor dear was desperate for a reliable vehicle.

She had a connection with a "friend and family" member of a Jeep dealer and they found her one. They delivered the vehicle to the Jeep dealer in Staunton. She arranged to go in and pay for the vehicle. I went with her. She was going to pay cash for it. Jeanne had one condition: they had to remove the front passenger seat.

The only reason they make right-hand drive vehicles in America is for rural route carriers. Jeanne thought it wasn't going to be a big deal. Well, there we were with the salesman in his little office with pictures of his kids on the wall.

When Jeanne asked if they had taken the seat out, he said, "Well, let me call the service desk and check in on that."

They called back. "It is going to be a problem because it was wired to the airbag and it would be another hundred dollars to take it out and it would take them a couple days to perform the task."

Oh, that pushed her button. She was ready to cancel the deal. But she was desperate and she agreed. We next went into the finance person's office to sign all the documents.

Jeanne wrote the check, we shook hands, and we were leaving to get into our car.

As we were about to enter our vehicle, the salesman came out and said he was sorry but there was a problem. The service people could not work on the Jeep until we actually drove the vehicle off the lot because she had not "taken possession" of the vehicle.

Oh my God. We were both steaming at this point. So for the first time Jeanne got into the new Jeep. I thought she was going to cry because she felt so "high" in the vehicle. In other words, she didn't think she could reach her mail boxes. That's why she couldn't sleep for weeks.

Jeanne drove the vehicle out of the parking lot and back into the lot so they could claim she had taken possession. This was more bureaucratic than the government.

A couple of days later, the dealer called and said removing the seat and canceling the airbag wiring would be three-hundred dollars instead of one-hundred dollars.

She told them to forget it and asked our neighbor mechanic Lindsey to do it.

So for weeks, Jeanne has been worried about the height of her seat and delivering mail to her five hundred–plus boxes. Saturday, we got the vehicle from Lindsey's shop to check mailboxes.

All the seats had been removed except the driver seat. I put a low-seat lounge chair in the passenger side. I had a clipboard and the pad of forms to let patrons know if their mailbox was not high enough for Jeanne to efficiently do her job.

Jeanne had a tape measure. We were going to measure every single mailbox . . . more than five hundred!

I had to use the handle over the window to lower myself into my low rider lounge chair. As soon as I sat down, the chair fabric ripped. My butt rested on the floor of the vehicle.

We proceeded with my head below the window, which made the onset of car sickness rather quick.

Jeanne stopped at the first mailbox. She leaned out the window with the measuring tape, measured the distance from the ground to the bottom of the box, and called out the height. It's supposed to be 42.5 inches from the ground.

We did this for every single mailbox. If they were too low, I filled out a form to leave in the mailbox requesting the patron fix the deficiency.

All told, about seventy-five boxes needed to be raised.

Coming out of Valley Mills subdivision, there is an extreme curve. I said, "Hey, this would be a good place to get out and move your mail trays forward."

"Get out? I just use the curve and slam on the brakes," she replied.

2015
Covey of Quail at the River

Today I went to the river and drove into the first crossing. When I stopped the truck, a covey of at least eight Northern Bobwhites burst to the south out of the lower wildlife area just below the culvert.

This is huge. I have not seen a covey of quail here since 2004. The wildlife experts keep saying pen-raised birds will not survive, much less reproduce. Well, I believe we have done it. Here is the secret: habitat, hope, and persistence.

2017
The Easement Holder Sold Us Out

A line in a great song: "There's only two things that money can't buy, and that's true love and homegrown tomatoes." There's another thing that money can't buy: trust.

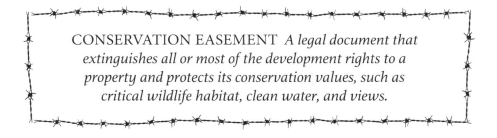

CONSERVATION EASEMENT *A legal document that extinguishes all or most of the development rights to a property and protects its conservation values, such as critical wildlife habitat, clean water, and views.*

When the Virginia Outdoors Foundation (VOF) accepted Dominion Energy's four-million dollar payoff to build its fracked-gas pipeline through eleven "eased" farms, they sold their soul and our trust. They betrayed the trust of every landowner who donated development rights to VOF since 1968 as well as all future donors. Those people gave them over eight hundred thousand acres of development rights to defend.

Dominion Energy wants to build a forty-two-inch, high-pressure, fracked-gas pipeline through West Virginia, Virginia, and North Carolina. The current planned route goes through eleven "eased" farms in Virginia. On Monday, October 16, 2017, the VOF granted Dominion Energy their "swap" of three parcels of land and blood money for the right to dig through these eleven farms.

VOF was in a tight spot. When the Federal Energy Regulatory Commission approved the Atlantic Coast Pipeline, it gave them the green light to use eminent domain. So Dominion Energy was going to "take" the land either way. Seemingly, there were two choices: Say no to the "swap" and get nothing in return, or take the "swap" and get the money.

They forgot about the value of trust. The trust every easement donor had and the trust that can never be regained for the future of open-space protection.

2008

November

I am so frustrated at work because processes, procedures, and protocol are crippling my ability to produce. Are the process people running our agency or are the progress people running the agency? Processes should enhance progress, not impede it.

2005
Pearly Gates Paint

Jeanne was frantic about finding more paint for the walls of Meadowview (in preparation for a garden club tour). All we had left, after every surface of the house was painted the same color years ago, was about an inch in the bottom of an old Ace Hardware paint can. She insisted that the name of the paint was "Pearly Gates" and insisted it was Sherwin Williams paint and that she had gotten it from the Sherwin Williams paint store on Greenville Avenue.

Off I went in search of the holy paint. When I arrived, the attendant said they never had paint by that name and he pointed to the can I brought in and asked why I didn't try Ace Hardware since it was in their can. The Duron Paint store was on the way to Ace, so I stopped in on the chance they were the carrier of the paint. I took the paint can in and asked if they had "Pearly Gates." The guy said he didn't think so and added that they didn't have the color "Gates of Hell" either. After a few laughs, the attendant said they had a "Pearly White" and he took a sample from the bottom of my old can and matched it up. It was their paint.

3
Winter

'Good Oak' Revisited

Aldo Leopold wrote eloquently about an ancient log he placed on the andirons of his fire in A Sand County Almanac, *published in 1949. The chapter was "Good Oak." Below is my lament for a log I placed on the andirons of a fire we had in the former slave house fireplace of Meadowview.*

I held the old log in my hands, and before I placed it on the fire, I reverently thought about the distinguished service that tree had provided and all the history it must have seen. It started putting on growth rings in 1619. That's the year the first representative government was formed in the New World, the House of Burgesses in Jamestown, Virginia. Coincidentally, it was the same year a Dutch ship brought the first Africans to Jamestown, launching the cruel system of slavery in Virginia.

The White Oak seedling was just germinating, and I'll bet the rabbits ate the new seedling for seven years before it had a root big enough to send up a shoot that could outgrow the height of rabbits in a single year. That would have been about 1625, the year King James I died.

The oak grew tall and straight for 125 years. It provided food and shelter for wildlife, sequestered tons of carbon, pumped tons of oxygen into the atmosphere, transpired thousands of gallons of water, and provided shade to the forest floor. Eastern Bison roamed under its branches and ate its acorns. Passenger Pigeons and Carolina Parakeets roosted in its branches. It saw Indian hunting parties, and it witnessed the first European settlers around 1725.

In 1750 the oak was selected to provide logs to build one of the first pioneer log cabins west of Staunton, which still stands within sight of our house. In the next century, most of the trees in the Valley would be cut to make way for agriculture and the new European way of life. The Eastern Bison, Passenger Pigeons, and Carolina Parakeets would become extinct.

By 1850 the Shenandoah Valley was the largest wheat producing region in the United States. In 1864 this cabin survived what historians call "The Burning." That's when Union general Philip Sheridan swept through the Valley burning the barns, mills, and cabins to help end the American Civil War. Within sight of this cabin the Yankees burned down the original Swoope Mill, which used water from Middle River for power.

My mother-in-law bought the log cabin in 2011 and restored it. It has big logs with narrow chinking and daubing, which is rare around here; most existing log cabins have little logs with wide chinking.

The two-foot-long log I held in my hands was part of a larger log that had to be taken out because it was infested with termites. It was replaced by a new oak log. That old termite-infested log served dutifully for 393 years. It was with great reverence that I placed this ancient stalwart of the earth on the fire where it would release the carbon it started sequestering in 1619. We raised a glass in its honor and watched the release of 393 years of history.

Frozen Cow Pies on Frozen Ground

There must be a thousand frozen cow pies on the ground. It has been unusually cold, and because of the snow, we've been feeding a lot of hay to the cows. Because they spend a lot of time where the hay is, it creates a dense pattern of dung on the already frozen snow.

The cow pies freeze and become hard as rocks—rocks as big as footballs.

This past year the passenger door of the hydra-bed truck broke and a neighboring farmer happened to have a spare door that fit perfectly. Farmers are very resourceful and never throw anything away. I can hear my neighbor now, "We better save that door; we might need it someday." It's nice having a door that closes without a lot of persuasion. I am known on the farm as "gate boy," which means I ride shotgun and open all the gates. I get in and out of the truck a lot. The broken door was a source of consternation for years. The only odd thing about the new door is that it's jet black. The rest of the truck is white.

Jeanne, five feet, four inches tall, can barely touch the pedals of this all-wheel-drive, six-wheelin' hydraulic monster, but much to my amazement she can feed the cows with this truck in the frozen snow. Most farmers in these snowy conditions would use a tractor. But not Jeanne; she is going to use a truck. To do this she has to drive fast, really fast. That's because she doesn't want to get stuck. Complicating matters is the multitude of frozen cow pies that are so prevalent that one cannot possibly drive a course that avoids them. So here's Jeanne's challenge: To drive fast enough on top of the frozen snow to avoid getting stuck yet slow enough to not cause damage to the truck or its passengers by the prevalent, unavoidable frozen cow pies. Because the frozen obstacles cannot be avoided and the cows must be fed, damage to the truck and its passengers ensues.

Jeanne's hard-driving spirit is well suited to the task as we haul ass over the frozen field. Here we are in this big farm truck with hydraulic arms; Jeanne is in her soiled farm clothes. It's all so rough and tough, yet this woman is so feminine. She has leather work gloves on and pearl earrings. I look down at her right foot stretching for all it's worth to reach the accelerator and notice the only thing touching the pedal is the very tip of her boot yet we travel at an ungodly speed, bumping violently over the rocks of dung. How can the end of such a small foot result in such speed?

Exacerbating my anxiety is the fact there is nothing to hold on to in this speeding massive feeding truck. Dexter, our faithful Border Collie, and I bounce uncontrollably and violently as we race to Jeanne's desired feeding location. I have seen Dexter's entire body in midair.

Ode to Dexter, Our Working Border Collie

Winter in Swoope. I walk along the banks of Middle River on our farm in search of treasure. Dexter, our Border Collie, used to walk along with me but he passed on, and I sure miss him. Cold air seeps through the opening in my collar; the brown, frozen grass crunches under my feet. The water in the river is clear today—that's because there are no cows in it upstream.

Dexter was one of my heroes. If only we could all be like him: fearless at work, tireless, always happy to see you, and playful; he was a great companion. I told people he was worth 1.5 men and 2.0 husbands. In retrospect, I think he was worth far more than that. We live and work on a beef cattle farm with 120 brood cows and their babies. He was our right arm. I saw him swing from a bull's tail one time when he was asked to bring the bulls in.

One of the famous Dexter stories is when Jeanne asked him to bring all six bulls in from the front field. It was June 1, the day we put

> **HERDING DOG COMMANDS** *On out: go out to the far side of the herd and bring the cows in. Away: go to the right of the herd. Come by: go to the left. Walk up: get closer to the herd. Steady: slow down. That will do: stop working and return.*

the bulls in with the cows. Dexter, Jeanne, and I walked through the barnyard, through the field with the round pen in it to the gate at the southwestern corner of the front field. She opened the gate and we walked through.

It was early morning; the knee-high grass was wet with dew. Dexter was smiling. I always thought he would rather work cattle than eat or play. His eyes were on Jeanne, eagerly waiting for a command.

"On out," she said as she pointed to the farthest bull.

All we could see was a small wave of green grass moving because the grass was taller than Dexter. The bull was at the other end of the field, and it was amazing to see this little wave of grass moving toward the big black bull just standing there over a hundred yards away. It took several minutes for Dexter to arrive a few feet behind the bull. There he stopped and waited for another command.

"Walk up!" Jeanne shouted. I don't know how he heard her, but he did, and a few seconds later the little green wave burst toward the bull's hind legs. Our hero nipped the leg of a bull weighing at least a ton. The bull immediately began trotting toward the gate.

It was a sight to see: Dexter working side to side to bring all six bulls through the gate and into the barnyard. He was wet, tired, and happy.

Never doubt that sixty-five pounds of fearless enthusiasm can move two thousand pounds of testosterone.

He died on January 28, 2016. His heart was bigger than ours will ever be.

I move on alone along the river bank. There is always treasure to be found.

A Snow Goose forages along with the Canada Geese in a neighbor's field. That's a rare sight around here. Thorns on the Hawthorn trees wait for shrikes to return. Our native Hawthorn is excellent habitat for them. We have not seen one since 2012. It's a mystery as to why they are gone. No doubt it's something we humans are doing.

I've noticed the resurgence of Virginia Wild Rye along the banks of the river. When the cows were in the river, I never saw this native plant. Now it has come to help anchor the soil and please the eye. It's one of the few native "cool season" grasses.

Time to go feed the cows. I feel Dexter herding me toward the truck.

Snowquester, Special Spots, and Short-Eared Owls

This past week Swoope bore the brunt of the Snowquester, a.k.a. winter storm "Saturn." It gave us almost two feet of snow—unwelcome weather for cattle farmers during calving season. A calf born in this weather can perish quickly. We were lucky. The storm left no casualties among our herds.

Snow still covers the land. Late yesterday afternoon we rode in the four-wheel-drive hydra-bed truck with a thousand-pound round bale of hay on it, through the snow, to give each herd plenty of hay. We also checked the cows for signs of labor and tagged any new babies.

As we checked the cows, we noticed cow tracks in the snow from cows leading to places along the fence or near a thicket of shrubs. These were cows looking for their "special spot" to have their babies: away from the other cows and somewhat protected from weather and predators. They select their spot, and then go back to the herd until the process of labor begins. Cow 75 was in her spot, so Jeanne unrolled a dab of hay for her. After the baby is born and gets his first meal the mama cow will tuck him into the dry hay to keep him warm.

It was sundown, and we were now finished with all the farm chores. We headed home to stoke the fire in the woodstove and relax a bit with a glass of wine.

One of our calving herds is behind the house to the west. Jeanne was looking out a window with binoculars checking the cows for signs of labor, and sure enough there was a cow on the horizon with her water bag out—the first real sign of active labor. We both watched the whole birth from the French door windows in the kitchen. The cow laid down for a while then stood up. Next, the front feet of the calf emerged; she laid down again, then stood up. A huge push and the head emerged. Now she was standing up with the baby halfway out dangling from her womb. Birth vapor rose from the baby still enveloped in the placenta. The mother spun around and pushed several more times, and minutes later the baby plopped onto the now freezing, snow-covered ground. The mother immediately began licking that baby with her huge warm tongue. In less than a minute the calf's head was up. It was the perfect bovine birth.

It wasn't quite dark, so we decided to check the other cows one more time from the road. Cow 75 was still in her special spot, most likely in labor. As we drove home on Cattleman Road just past dusk, we stopped to watch the Short-Eared Owls hunt. I thought how difficult it would be for them in this snow to find a mouse or a Meadow Vole. The voles especially like snow because it creates an opaque shield from the many raptors that prey on them—especially owls.

We were lucky. Two owls emerged from mystery and hunted stealthily over the snow-covered grasslands of Swoope. We watched them with our binoculars until our arms ached. They flap their wings silently then glide over the snow-covered runways the voles make in these vast grasslands.

These owls dive feet first for prey, and one of them caught something under the snow. Its wings were splayed horizontally on top of the snow. Its head went under the snow, and it took a bite of its prey; then it popped its head up and spun it around in one direction almost 180 degrees and then spun it the other way. We didn't leave until it was too dark to see.

The grasslands of Swoope are home to many special creatures. Birders from all over Virginia come here to see the Short-Eared Owls. The owls are here because of the Meadow Voles and the voles are here because of the grass. Cows are another special creature, and during the next few months many cows will be searching for a special spot to have their babies.

Winter Storm 'Thor' and a New Puppy

The sun's energy has transformed our brown pastures into green carpets of food for our beef cattle. The surge of spring is upon us. Red-Winged Blackbird males are singing their shoulders off: "Concareeee." Meadowlarks are singing, "Spring of the yearrrr." Because of the extensive grasslands in Swoope, their populations are not declining here. Elsewhere they are, along with other grassland species of birds.

It's calving season on the farm. We have eighty-three calves on the ground; eight heifers (young cows that have never had a baby) to go and nineteen cows.

By the time winter storm Thor arrived on March 5, six cows had calved and snow covered the ground. Eight calves were born during the storm. It was the worst possible weather for calving; thirty-one degrees with snow and freezing rain.

During the storm, Cow 116 delivered her baby, unbeknownst to her, into a groundhog hole. He never got up. When we found him, he was in the process of dying from hypothermia. We brought him in and placed him in the calf cooker. After about seven hours in the cooker he warmed up enough to begin a calf's instinctual sucking motion with its mouth; time for him to go back to his mother. We fed him a bottle of colostrum to jump-start him, loaded him in the tractor, and dropped him near his anxiously waiting mother.

They literally hooked up, mouth to teat, in less than a minute. Several weeks later we noticed the ends of his ears had frozen off so his head looks just like a mouse. We nicknamed him Mickey, after Mickey Mouse.

Another calf, Red Tag 121, also born in the storm, lost part of his left ear. Most likely a cow stepped on his ear while he was sleeping and as he jerked awake, the tag and part of his ear came off, making it sort of pointed. We call him Spock.

Cow Y99 successfully delivered twins on March 17. She knew they were both hers but favored only one. She would smell and lick the second one but wouldn't let him nurse. Jeanne tried for two days to get her to accept both babies. As a distraction, a pan of grain was offered while Jeanne positioned the hungry baby at the teat.

Jeanne does magic with cattle, and they trust her. She milked the cow right in the field and trained the unwanted baby to nurse. After two days, the mother still did not accept the second baby without grain. He's now a bottle baby in the barn enjoying three meals a day.

We have a new addition to our family: a Border Collie puppy, Valentino, or Val for short. His mother hails from a working sheep farm in Highland County, Virginia, and his father hails from our neighbor's cattle farm in Swoope, Virginia. He is fitting right in.

Cows, Calves, and Cranes

Earth awakens from the cold during the month of March in America's legendary Shenandoah Valley. Days lengthen, migrations begin, chloroplasts awaken and absorb the energy from the sun's photons—photosynthesis begins. Pastures slowly turn from brown to green. Life's energy is on the move.

March. The end of winter and the beginning of spring. It usually brings the most severe weather, and it's our busiest month on the farm because we begin calving. One hundred and thirty-eight pregnant cows are all due to give birth in the next ninety days.

Red-Winged Blackbirds arrived in Swoope at the end of February, and that, for me, signals the beginning of the great avian migration. Each day I look for a new arrival. A Fox Sparrow one day, Hooded Mergansers and Buffleheads another, an Osprey. Killdeers amass. Bluebirds start looking into the nest boxes we put up for them and for other cavity nesters.

Each day we feed the cows, we check a nearby pond for migrating birds. Bald Eagles nest nearby. One day as we drove slowly across the dam, I scanned the far end of the pond and—oh my God—there were several Sandhill Cranes. Sandhill Cranes are very rare for Swoope. They are on their way to breed in Canada, above the Arctic Circle.

4
Spring

Spring Surge in Swoope and the Arrival of Tree Swallows

There is a special day each spring that is magical. That's the first day of the year I notice the earth is really on the move. It's not necessarily the day the first daffodil blooms or the first warm day of spring. It's a day when the energy of life seems to be surging in every creature. Every bird is singing, plants are growing, snakes are sunning, and bees are buzzing. You can see it, hear it, smell it, and feel it. We don't have a word for it, but I know when it happens. This day often corresponds to the day most students skip school. I call this "Spring Surge Day," and in Swoope, Virginia, it's usually the day Tree Swallows arrive from Central America to stake out their nesting territories.

All swallows that we see in the temperate region of America are neotropical migrants. This means they winter in the tropics and migrate north to nest and raise their young. Tree Swallows have traveled more than a thousand miles to get here. Their summer range is expanding north and they have been arriving earlier almost every year since I have lived in Swoope.

This year the swallows arrived on February 24. Last year they arrived on February 28, the year before, they arrived on March 8, and three years ago they arrived on March 14. It doesn't take ice core samples from Antarctica and NASA data to convince me that we are getting warmer earlier. We can use just plain old scientific observation.

Flood Plains and Soil Regulate the Water Cycle

Here in Swoope, we've had ten and a half inches of rain over the past three days.

Our part of Middle River has been out in its floodplain for the third day in a row. Flood waters have completely covered much of the pasture in the river field and the fence that keeps our cattle out of the river. When the river gets back into its banks we will walk along the fence and clean debris off the wire.

When the river started expanding into the floodplain, we moved the cattle out of the river field to higher ground. Thank goodness, we only have one strand of electric fence along the river. Fences in floodplains have always been a troublesome issue.

One must either keep the fence out of a river's raging waters or put up the least amount of fence that will work. For us, a single strand of electric wire along the river works just fine.

Floodplains and soils are great hydrologic features. Together they provide one of the most important environmental services on earth, that of regulating the water cycle.

Floodplains slow the velocity of raging flood waters. Once slowed, the sediments suspended in the water can settle out and deposit on the underlying land. Some of the most productive soils in the world were created by these deposits. Water-deposited soils are called alluvial soils and they are often referred to as river-bottom soils.

Dry soils are like big sponges; they absorb rainwater. Gravity pulls this water downward and soil particles and organic matter in the soil filter the water before it eventually ends up in our groundwater. Without soil, there would be no filter to recharge the groundwater.

Soils can only absorb so much water, and once the "filter" is full, water begins to run off. If the soil is not anchored down with plants, it will be vulnerable to the energy of the flowing water, which will

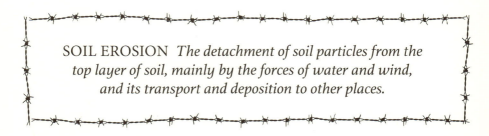

SOIL EROSION *The detachment of soil particles from the top layer of soil, mainly by the forces of water and wind, and its transport and deposition to other places.*

carry it away. This is soil erosion. The brown color seen in flood water was once productive soil on someone's farm. After it washes away and enters a stream, it becomes the largest water pollutant, by volume, on the earth. What one farmer upstream loses to the forces of erosion will become productive soil in a floodplain downstream or nonpoint source water pollution.

Today the sun is out and the river will go back into its channel. We will walk along our streamside fence and shake off the debris. It's part of how we live with the river on a cattle farm.

The Quail Survive

May fills my senses as I walk our river field. Life's energy surges this time of year. The avian migration is at its peak. All the birds that want to be here have arrived except for the Dickcissels. They will arrive when the peonies and day lilies open.

The cool nights and warm days have forced the Orchardgrass and bluegrass in our pastures and hayfields to head out, which means the seed heads are emerging from the uppermost leaf sheath. The cows munch. The calves are muscular and quick, with their mother's milk smudged on their heads.

My boots and jeans are wet from dew all the way up to my knees.

There is not a moment without birdsong. It used to torment me not knowing who was singing, but now I know. Robins, Cardinals, Warbling Vireos, Yellow Warblers, Bobolinks, Grasshopper

Sparrows, Meadowlarks, Red-Winged Blackbirds, and Baltimore Orioles all singing at one time. The avian symphony plays constantly this time of year.

I walk along the bottom of a steep, wooded slope in search of the quail we released last fall. I heard them the other day singing their "Hoy-ee" song. I see a male nervously walking under the thorny Hawthorn trees, and farther away I spot two females. They made it through the long, cold, wet winter. Mate my friends. Beat the odds and give us renewed hope. It was ten years ago that I last saw a covey here in this very place.

Wild Cherry and Black Willow trees are in full bloom. False Indigo Bush and River Birch are budding out. I walk to the river's edge where the cattle used to cross. It is amazing how quickly Mother Nature can heal eroding stream banks once the cattle are removed. She planted a Sycamore tree right in the middle of the north side of the crossing. It grew much faster than the ones we planted. Its roots anchor the soil and its leaves provide food for insects that live in the water.

The river is swollen and milk-chocolate brown gurgling past the Sycamore. It carries the wealth from farms upstream. What was the most productive soil on a farm upstream clogs the gills of the Mayflies and smothers the eggs of the trout that would be here. This sediment and all that is attached to it are what separate us from a healthy river and a restored Chesapeake Bay.

I lament that I have not done more . . . and walk on.

A flash of blue flies past that lifts my heart: it's an Indigo Bunting nesting in the shrubs we planted. I see a Tree Swallow carry small white feathers into one of the nest boxes we put up. Another one sits on the fence, ever vigilant to protect the nest.

I check another nest box for eggs. Baby Tree Swallows have already hatched.

The surge of life's energy is at its peak during the month of May here in Swoope.

Bobwhites, Bobolinks, and Black Locust Blooms

May might be my favorite month. The energy of spring swells in every living thing. I remain in awe of all the energy. A Catbird sings all night outside our open window. Robins begin their singing at 5:15 a.m. That's the warm-up for the avian symphony that will last all day. I heard a Blackpoll Warbler in the yard this morning as squadrons of Chimney Swifts flew overhead. When the Blackpoll passes through on its way to the Arctic to breed, the other late migrants should be here as well: Yellow Billed Cuckoos and Dickcissels.

I hear Bobolinks and Bobwhites every day here in Swoope. The Bobolinks have the craziest song I have ever heard from a bird (Bobolinks have a double larynx), and they are so strikingly beautiful in their black-and-white tuxedos with little yellow helmets. They will nest in our cool-season pastures along with the Eastern Meadowlarks and Grasshopper Sparrows.

Last month we released fifty Northern Bobwhites on four different farms in Swoope. We now have a pair in the yard and at least another male in the pasture to the north. Our neighbor has a pair as well. Will we see their chicks this year? We hope so. Shrubby habitat and native landscapes are key to bringing their populations back.

Our cows will not be able to keep up with the growth of the forage in the pastures. Orchardgrass has already headed out and is in anthesis—that's when the anthers are out emitting their pollen into the air. I tell Jeanne, "That hay ought to be in the barn." She gives me the ol' one-eye look, meaning she doesn't like me bringing up the subject. We both know we'd never get it cured because of the rains and cool temperatures. Nevertheless, from a nutritional standpoint, it should be in the barn.

Orchardgrass, fescue, bluegrass, and Tall Meadow Oat Grass are all in bloom emitting pollen, which in many people causes an allergic reaction called hay fever. They don't really get a fever, but the runny nose and itchy eyes are their body's reaction to the pollen emitted by the plants that farmers grow for hay.

The Black Locust trees are in full bloom. They are totally white with flowers. I can hear the bees on those blooms from afar; it's like an interstate highway for pollinators. The flowers are an important source for honey.

This native tree is awesome. It's in the pea family and like all legumes produces its own nitrogen. Farmers use the timber from this tree for fence posts because the wood is very resistant to rot and the wood is dense, making it ideal for firewood. This tree is also what we call a "pioneer" species, which means it is one of the first trees to establish in abandoned fields. For wildlife, pollinators, utilitarian value, and beauty, it's one of our great native trees.

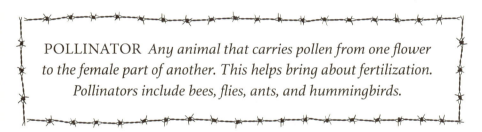

POLLINATOR *Any animal that carries pollen from one flower to the female part of another. This helps bring about fertilization. Pollinators include bees, flies, ants, and hummingbirds.*

Fox Kits, Frogs, and Warbler Fallout

We live on a farm in the headwaters of the Shenandoah River, a tributary of the Chesapeake Bay. How cool is that? We started this year's calving season on March 1 with 122 pregnant beef cows. All except nine have calved. Cows 65 and X6 had twins.

I write this on Earth Day, and the rising temperatures of April accelerate the surge of spring. Living and working on a farm gives me many opportunities to experience special moments, those times when you are still and quiet and can breathe in the surge of spring.

There's a Red Fox den in one of the pastures. Each day when I check on the cows, I can see a couple of kits playing near their holes in the land. I call it a fox "hotel" because of all the holes. A parent fox always watches me from a distance. The kits peek out of their holes as I watch. There are five kits this year. One time I saw all five playing, like a bunch of kittens rolling around on each other.

In the early evenings when the farm chores are completed, I usually sit on the patio under the towering branches of the Silver Maple and Southern Pecan trees and wait for one of those special

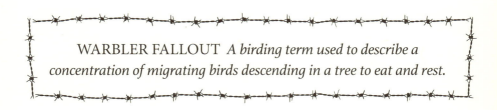

WARBLER FALLOUT *A birding term used to describe a concentration of migrating birds descending in a tree to eat and rest.*

moments. Today I see two American Green Frogs staring at me from the small concrete pond we have near the patio. They don't move. They are the ones that sound like a banjo string being plucked.

This time of year is my favorite because of the avian migration. Every couple of days a new migrant passes through or arrives. It starts with the Red-Winged Blackbirds in February, then Chipping Sparrows, then Tree Swallows. Now it's warblers, those tiny gems of the treetops. Today, Earth Day 2016, I witnessed the first warbler fallout at Meadowview. The moment I was waiting for had arrived.

I couldn't see them at first, but I heard them: that cascading melodious song. Warbler songs used to drive me crazy when I did not know what they were. But now, after much study, I can bird by ear. It must be the Yellow-Rumped Warbler, I thought. Way up in the top of the towering tree branches, I see tiny birds flitting around. Binos in hand, I wait for one of the specks to land. They will be still for only a split second. There it is. Yes, Yellow-Rumped Warbler. A whole bunch of them.

The Yellow-Rumped Warbler is a five-and-a-half-inch bird of the treetops. Flocks of them are passing through Swoope on their way perhaps to Canada to breed for the summer. It is indeed a special moment to have them visit here in Swoope.

Blackpoll Warblers in Swoope

Blackpoll Warblers came to the trees in our yard this week. I don't know a lot of people who have seen one, and when I mention Blackpolls I get funny stares—I'm a birder.

These tiny birds, barely five inches long, migrate this time of year from South America all the way to the boreal forests in Canada. They're just passing through Swoope and the rest of the mid-Atlantic flyway right now, and it is a real treat to hear and see one of these long-distance travelers.

It's a spiritual connection for me when I see a visitor like the Blackpoll Warbler in the backyard; it is one of the millions of birds in the Great Avian Migration that we know so little about. The Blackpoll Warbler represents the tail end of the migration—it's almost over. Most of the neotropical migrants are now on their nesting grounds for the season.

I see Blackpolls every year because I can hear them. They have a distinctive buzzing song, and as soon as I hear them, I can locate them with my binoculars. The first one I ever saw was while I was in

NEOTROPICAL MIGRATOR *A bird that breeds and nests in North America during the summer but winters in Central and South America. It flies long distances to take advantage of seasonally abundant food.*

the parking lot of the liquor store in Staunton, Virginia. My birding mentor at the time had me listen to the Blackpoll's high-pitched buzzing song, and sure enough there they were, up in the trees over the parking lot.

Sixty percent of the birds you hear in Virginia in May are migratory birds; they are only here for the summer nesting season. The birds are singing because they are in breeding mode, looking for a mate and a territory to raise their young. By August they will have completed their mission and will begin their long journey back to their wintering grounds in warmer climates.

5
Summer

Fireflies, Soldier Beetles, and Farmscape

Several years ago, we took in two ladies who needed a place to stay. They were from Wyoming. One had just quit her job; I think she was running away from something. We agreed to put them up for a couple of weeks until they could find a place of their own. It was late June and we were sitting on the grand porch here at Meadowview about dusk. They had never seen Fireflies before.

"What's that?" one of them exclaimed, observing the flickering yellow tail light of the beetle.

"Oh my God!" The other one said.

By ten o'clock there were thousands of tiny, yellow flickering lights all over the yard, in the trees, over the horizon... everywhere. Couple this bio-fireworks event with some heat lightning and rumbling thunder in the distance, and you have a show worthy of the gods.

Fireflies or lightning bugs are true beetles. They are beneficial insects. Not only do they put on a great show in the evenings, they prey on many harmful insects in the garden during their larval stage of life in the soil and as adults. During their larval stage, they eat slugs and other soil insect larvae. During their adult stage, they also eat soft-bodied insects such as aphids and Colorado Potato Beetle larvae.

We have perennial plant beds around our vegetable garden to attract beneficial insects such as the Fireflies, Soldier Beetles, Lady Bugs, Lacewings, Syrphid Flies, and Praying Mantises. Gardeners call these perennial beds insectaries or farmscapes. The insects need a place to hang out. They like places with lots of different plants in different stages of development. A farmscape is simply a variety of different flowering plants like Yarrow, Queen Ann's Lace, Goldenrod, Coneflower and Black-Eyed Susan. The more plants you have, especially native ones, the more beneficial insects you will have.

Fireflies and Soldier Beetles are the Tyrannosaurus Rexes of the insect world. There aren't any aphids on our tomatoes or beetles on the potatoes because of these and other beneficial insects.

Fireflies never cease to amaze me. Jeanne and I were driving home late one night, and we came upon the wildlife area of a neighbor's farm. It was a "stop the car" moment. Tens of thousands of Fireflies were in action over the weeds on the wildlife side of the road. The other side of the road, where the pasture was grazed fairly close, had hardly any Fireflies at all. Some folks hate the neighbor's wildlife area because it has so many weeds. They say it's full of trash and filth, but it's jam-packed full of biodiversity.

Tomatoes, Bobwhites, and Middle River Flowing Like Chocolate Milk

Corn is tasseling, and we are eating tomatoes from the garden at every meal. Tomato sandwiches for breakfast, gazpacho for lunch, and sliced tomatoes for dinner. My favorite varieties this year are Black Krim and Mr. Stripey. They are the silkiest and juiciest, and they are not mealy at all. Each day for breakfast, Jeanne and I eat tomato sandwiches. She toasts Wonder Bread and I toast Arnold's Healthy Multi-Grain. When the bread is just turning brown we take the warm slices out of the toaster, put a layer of mayo on the bread then a slice of tomato that's at least as thick as the bread, add salt, and devour. "Oh my God, this is good," is our tomato prayer repeated every morning after the first bite.

Gazpacho, zucchini soup, grilled squash, corn on the cob, okra, and peppers are regulars for dinner. When we harvest more tomatoes than we can eat or give away, we make sauce.

A few of the Northern Bobwhites we released in October are still alive. I hear them calling every day and search for them, hoping to see babies. I've got this hope thing going. If we release enough birds and keep doing it every year, maybe, just maybe, a pair will reproduce and contradict all the bureaucrats and scientists that say it can't be done.

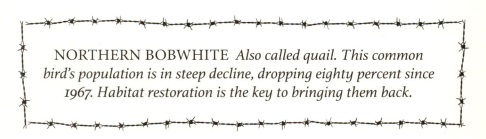

NORTHERN BOBWHITE *Also called quail. This common bird's population is in steep decline, dropping eighty percent since 1967. Habitat restoration is the key to bringing them back.*

I look for Bobwhites at our river field where most of their habitat is. We fenced the cows out of the river and two tributaries many years ago. As I walk along the river I can hear a male Bobwhite calling at the fringe of the old woods. I make my way to the river's edge through the tall weeds. The river looks like milk chocolate flowing. It's brown because of all the cows standing in the river upstream. When they enter or exit the river, their hooves destroy the banks, dislodging soil that then enters the water. The soil they dislodge clouds the water and clogs the gills of the insects that live there.

When cows hang out in the river, they also excrete urine and manure. This puts nutrients, fecal coliform, and pathogens that can cause leptospirosis, cryptosporidiosis, and other diseases in the water. Not only can our cows get whatever disease the herd upstream has, but we humans can get some of these diseases as well.

The sediment dislodged by the upstream cows and the nutrients, pathogens, and hormones they excrete also have a profound negative impact on the health of the water, livestock, and people downstream. We have a plan and the money to fix this. It's called the Chesapeake Clean Water Blueprint.

Fencing livestock from streams is the most effective and, by far, the least expensive way to improve the health of streams.

Solar Panels Radiate Hope in Swoope

"Solar panels are only forty percent efficient," he said.

"Are you kidding? So what? It's free," I thought.

The sun shines and zap, you have electricity, isn't that one-hundred-percent efficient? Well, not really. The forty percent rating is true if one thinks about how scientists measure efficiency—the actual number of photons hitting a photovoltaic cell and being converted to electricity. Scientists have only been able to convert forty percent of the sunlight into electricity in a lab. We purchased the highest-efficiency photovoltaic panels on the market, and they are only sixteen percent efficient.

More to the Story on Solar

So many other factors should enter the scientists' woefully simplistic expression of efficiency. With solar energy, there are no costs for the extraction or transportation of sunlight. There is no byproduct from the use of sunlight and no accidental damage, and there are no resource protection costs for rays of sun. Nor are there associated costs for healthcare or environmental damages as there are for fossil fuel energy sources.

- Think how much it costs to mine coal, drill for oil, frack for gas, or mine uranium. There are no extraction costs with solar rays.

- Other forms of energy require transportation: train cars filled with coal, tankers filled with crude oil, pipelines filled with gas. Not so with solar; the rays hitting our photovoltaic cells require no transportation costs.
- The cost of waste disposal with fossil fuels and nuclear is significant, requiring space and oversight to protect us and the environment from faulty engineering, sloppy construction, or corruption.
- Accidents abound with coal, natural gas, and oil. The Upper Big Branch Coal Mine explosion in West Virginia, the San Bruno natural gas pipeline explosion, the BP oil spill, and the Dan River coal ash spill quickly come to mind.
- What are the costs to protect and defend our foreign interests in oil or its transport? I think about the pirates off the Somali coast, the Gulf War, and protecting the Suez Canal. We don't need special forces or a Department of Defense to protect our interests in solar power.
- Health care costs related to fossil fuel energy are far reaching; from black lung disease to asthma. One Harvard study states, "The life cycle effects of coal and the waste stream generated are costing the U.S. public a third to over one-half of a trillion dollars annually."

If energy efficiency factored in all these aforementioned associated costs, solar would be at or near the most cost-efficient.

Solar rays are free and unlimited. There are no moving parts and there are no greenhouse gases emitted from photovoltaic cells.

Downsides to Solar

The upfront cost is high but dropping fast. In 1975 the cost of a solar panel was $101.15 per watt; in 2017 a solar panel cost $0.37 per watt, according to Bloomberg and Earth Policy Institute. Just like hand-held calculators and computers, the start-up costs were high and then plummeted as markets adjusted and the industry advanced.

Solar panels take up space if they are not mounted on a roof. And, of course, if the sun isn't shining, little or no power is generated, so to be completely independent, the system requires batteries. Lack of storage capacity is a drawback, but here also, technology is improving and prices are falling.

Certainly, the manufacture of photovoltaic cells and the disposal of spent panels generate some pollution and waste, but the industry is so young, there is little data to reflect true costs.

These negative aspects pale in comparison to the downsides of fossil fuel and nuclear energy use.

Four Reasons We Went Solar

1. The Atlantic Coast Pipeline and gigantic transmission towers were our tipping points. The arrogance and disrespectful manner in which Dominion Power and Duke Energy are carrying out their plan to construct a six-hundred-mile, forty-two-inch, high-pressure, fracked-gas pipeline through America's legendary Shenandoah Valley, the place where we live, drove us to seek energy independence.
2. The "solarize 'your county' movement" in Virginia woke us up to the growing number of people going solar. Fifty people had signed up in Augusta County when we considered doing so, and we thought if we wanted to go solar and have the system up and running before the thirty percent federal tax credit expired, we had better get going.
3. We found the right place. The roof on our home would not work because it's not facing south, so we needed to build a ground array. Altenergy Staunton Branch Manager Joe Moore came out to our home and helped us find the right place, and it fit.
4. Finally, we want to do everything we can to reduce our personal carbon footprint.

Our Solar System

Altenergy built us a 7.56 kilowatt ground array with twenty-four SolarWorld panels, which is calculated to generate slightly more than our current energy needs. We will "net meter" for now, which means our utility company will give us credit for any electricity we contribute to the grid. We plan to go completely off the grid eventually.

Our solar setup and the folks at Altenergy exceeded our expectations. We were informed of every detail, they were courteous, cleaned up every day, and delivered what they promised.

The solar energy sector is exploding. In the United States a home or business goes solar every two and a half minutes. As the solar industry continues to grow, prices will come down.

Carbon and Catalpa

In June, the evenings are cool, and we love to sit on the porch with a glass of wine at dusk and wait for the Little Brown Bats to drop out of the bat house. As we wait, we hear Robins fuss and a Catbird meowing as they settle in for the evening. Hundreds of Fireflies flicker their tail lights in the distance. The first bat drops out of the box ten feet straight down, and then lifts off in flight to feed on multitudes of insects throughout the night. Then another, then two more, then another until all seventeen have dropped out.

June is also the beginning of the farm year for our cow and calf operation in the Shenandoah Valley. It's when the bulls go in with our three herds of cows. And June is when we make all the hay to feed the cows for the entire winter.

Harvesting Carbon

June is when we harvest carbon—the carbon sequestered by the grasses we cut for hay. We cut the grasses in our hay fields, let it dry, then bale it into half-ton round bales that we'll feed our cows this winter when the pastures are dormant. I love the smell of hay. For some odd reason, I love moving it out of the fields and storing it in the barn or in various caches throughout the farm. It's a wonderful feeling; knowing you have food for the cows for the entire winter. I like to think of making hay as baling sunshine. After all, sunlight and green plants make it possible for us to make hay and for all humanity to live.

Photons and Chloroplasts

A photon from a ray of sunshine hits a chloroplast in a leaf and the journey begins—photosynthesis: the most profound of all ecosystem services. Photosynthesis comes from Greek words meaning putting together from light. This process provides virtually all our food either directly or indirectly and virtually all our oxygen. In a nutshell, plants take in carbon dioxide and water and use the sun's energy to convert it into carbohydrates. In the process, plants release oxygen into the air. And the world turns.

Catalpa: Runway for Bees

Catalpa trees are in full bloom. They never cease to amaze me. The white, orchid-like, perfect flowers almost completely cover the tree during June.

They are a superhighway for pollinators. Standing near a tree at the river, I can hear hundreds of pollinators: bees, moths, bugs, flies. It's no wonder: the fragrance and flower design are magnets to them. The blossom is huge with a runway pattern of yellow and maroon to guide pollinators into the sweet spot where all the nectar and pollen reside.

The Catalpa is often called Indian Cigar Tree because of its long seed pods or beans it produces in the fall. It is a native, pioneer tree that is an excellent riparian buffer tree. It is a host-specific plant for the Catalpa Sphinx Moth, which is often parasitized by wasps. The immature stage of the moth, is a caterpillar, which makes excellent fish bait, and there are farms that grow Catalpa trees just to harvest the worms for bait.

In 1736, colonial Virginia's Royal Governor William Gooch planted two rows of Catalpa trees to line the Palace Green in Tidewater, Virginia. They were replanted in 1937 and stand today as a testament to their beauty and grandeur.

6
Fall

Figs and Fall Warblers

For the first time in my life, we harvested figs, which means we either got lucky or the planet is warming. We slice them in half and eat them fresh with a dab of creamy blue cheese while sipping a full-bodied, peppery Cabernet Sauvignon. Pair that with a burnt orange sunset over the Allegheny Mountains with trees starting to put on their kaleidoscope of fall color, and you have a classic fall afternoon in Swoope—welcome to Meadowview.

We put the vegetable garden to bed except for a few remaining pepper plants and a couple of tomato plants we have high hopes for. A thick blanket of Crimson Clover now covers the rich soil to protect it from the erosive force of falling raindrops. It's also a stimulus package for the soil microbes. Root growth and microbial activity help build healthy soil.

At the river, I witnessed a warbler wave. That's when a flock of these small birds passes through on its way to Central and South America. We planted some thickets of False Indigo Bush and alder a couple of years ago, and wouldn't you know it, that's where the long-distance travelers were: Nashville and Palm Warblers. Common Yellowthroats, a Northern Cardinal, a Carolina Wren, and some Song Sparrows joined them.

A Bald Eagle flew overhead.

Fall Asters, Boneset, Marsh Marigolds, Jewelweed, and Grand Lobelia are blooming in the wildlife corridors we established along the small streams. More trees have come up on their own in addition to the ones we planted. Catalpa, Green Ash, Black Walnut, Red Maple, and Sycamores are the native ones that we don't have to plant. I noticed the leaves on one of the Catalpas were being eaten by something. I got close and turned a leaf over—Catalpa Sphinx Moth caterpillars! There must be a thousand of them on this one tree. These are the ones they use for fish bait down South. I think I'll gather a bunch and feed them to the chickens.

We now wait for the White-Crowned Sparrows that will arrive with the frost in the coming days. The frost will make the Tall Fescue in the pastures more palatable for the cattle because the plant makes more sugars in cold weather. The calves are looking really good. They should average at least six hundred pounds when we sell them in December; they gain all that weight on good pasture, momma's milk, and my wife's patient and ever-watchful care.

Smoke will be going up the chimney soon. The violent windstorm in June left us with plenty of seasoned firewood to keep us warm all winter.

What Is a Tree Hugger?

The term "tree hugger" is synonymous with "environmental wacko." One might say it's used for environmental profiling.

From the dictionary: Tree hugger is a noun used informally, chiefly derogatory, for an environmental campaigner. I think I fit this description, although I believe in harvesting mature trees and weeding out undesirable trees by using sound forestry practices.

For hardwood timber, mature trees should be harvested through selective cutting methods. Clear-cutting a forest may have a place in the production of softwood such as Loblolly Pine, but in a hardwood forest dominated by oaks, hickory, and walnut, selective cutting is the best way to ensure a sustainable forest. After all, trees are renewable. So from a silvicultural standpoint, I'm not a tree hugger. I am, however, an environmental campaigner.

There are many reasons to not harvest a mature tree. For instance, we should not cut down genetically superior trees or ones that have the genetic traits we seek. That would be like killing the goose that laid the golden eggs. Harvest the seeds and nuts from these to plant new forests. We should also protect trees of remarkable significance such as the tallest, the oldest, or ones that have touched us in some way or connect us to history or a loved one. I am drawn to these trees and will often give them, yes, I admit it, a hug.

This year I gave two trees a hug: the Lafayette Sycamore on the Brandywine Battlefield of Pennsylvania and the Algernourne Live Oak in Fort Monroe, Virginia. I also reverently picked up a leaf from the famous American Chestnut tree known as the Thompson tree in Lesesne State Forest of Nelson County, Virginia. I would have hugged that tree, but it's fenced off to prevent the spread of a soil-born pathogen known as Black Ink Disease among American Chestnuts.

The Lafayette Sycamore

During our War of Independence (1776–81), the nineteen-year-old Marquis de Lafayette was wounded in the Battle of Brandywine. Legend has it they brought him to rest under this tree.

The Algernourne Live Oak

The Algernourne Live Oak is 474 years old. It's in Fort Monroe, now a national monument. This tree witnessed the first slaves entering the New World from Africa. The *White Lion*, a Dutch ship, landed here in 1619 when the port was called Old Point Comfort.

Fort Monroe, also known as the "Gibraltar of the Chesapeake," is the largest stone fortress in America. It was built to protect the Chesapeake Bay from invasion by sea. During the Civil War the fort was part of the Underground Railroad. It was a safe haven for runaway slaves because it was a Union stronghold within Virginia, a Confederate state. Harriet Tubman worked here, and Jefferson Davis, president of the Confederate States of America, was imprisoned here after the war.

The Thompson Tree

Until the twentieth century, the American Chestnut was the greatest tree in North America. Once the tallest, fastest-growing, and most dominant tree in the East, it was and still is the victim of an invasive fungus from Asia. In perhaps the greatest environmental disaster in America, these former mighty giants of the forest were reduced to mere stump sprouts that grow and die back every few years from the effects of the fungus called Chestnut Blight. The American Chestnut Foundation, with six thousand members, has a mission to restore the tree to our eastern forests.

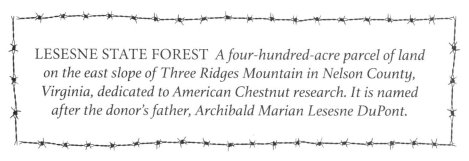

LESESNE STATE FOREST *A four-hundred-acre parcel of land on the east slope of Three Ridges Mountain in Nelson County, Virginia, dedicated to American Chestnut research. It is named after the donor's father, Archibald Marian Lesesne DuPont.*

According to some scientists, the Thompson Tree is one of the most blight-resistant American Chestnuts. It survives in the Lesesne State Forest in Nelson County, Virginia, which is dedicated to American Chestnut research. This tree is steeped in research history. Its roots grew from a radiation-treated nut planted during the Atomic Age sometime in the 1950s, when scientists used radioactive material to cause mutations. Years later researchers grafted true American Chestnut scion wood onto these roots. In addition, researchers infected the tree with hypovirulent strains of the fungus to increase the tree's resistance to the blight.

Thousands of people are dedicated to bringing back the American Chestnut to its former range; it's a true marriage of science and passion. Someday, the tree will regain its status as a mighty giant of the Eastern forest.

Fueling Stations for Monarchs

I had to stop and smell the marigolds, the native ones in our riparian buffers called Bur Marigolds. As I was putting up a new solar fence charger for one of our livestock exclusion areas, I had to just stop to watch. What froze me in my tracks was the sight of so many Monarch butterflies—those bright, orange-and-black, migrating ballerinas—fluttering about the flowers.

As I stood there motionless, more and more Monarchs came into focus. They would probe for nectar on one flower, and then flap their delicate wings and float to another. There must have been thirty or forty of them dancing among the flowers; a kaleidoscope of orange, black, yellow, and green. I could hear the buzzing sounds of other pollinators. Bumblebees, flies, and Ruby-Throated Hummingbirds, along with the Monarchs, were having a feast on the wild native flowers in the riparian buffer.

Native Flowers Feed the Monarchs

Bright yellow Bur Marigolds dominated the buffer, followed by the orange blooms of Jewelweed and the white blooms of Boneset. All these are native to the Valley; we didn't plant them. They just came on their own once we fenced the cattle out of the riparian areas. The pollen and nectar of these flowers and many others such as Ironweed, Grand Lobelia, Goldenrod, and Fall Aster provide much-needed nourishment for the pollinators.

Monarchs are fueling up to travel all the way to the fir forests in Mexico. Some migrate from Canada to Mexico, a journey of 2,500 miles. They are the only insect to migrate this far.

They have four life stages and four generations in one year. The fourth generation, the one I was mesmerized by, is the one that migrates to Mexico.

Monarch Caterpillars Eat Only Milkweed Leaves

When the fourth generation Monarchs journey north in the spring, they lay their eggs only on plants in the milkweed family. The emerging caterpillars eat only leaves of milkweed plants. The riparian areas on our farm have many native plants including hundreds, perhaps thousands, of milkweed plants such as Common Milkweed and Butterfly Weed.

Riparian buffers are the most important areas for wildlife because they provide food, shelter, and water. The leaves from native plants also feed the critters in the aquatic ecosystem. Jeanne and I are proud not only that we produce quality food for people but also that our land cleanses overland flow of water and provides habitat for wildlife. We produce food, clean water, and fueling stations for Monarchs. We are part of a growing number of farmers who improve their soil and water to restore our river—Middle River—and the Chesapeake Bay.

Sipping Africa, Mandela, and the Reality of Trump

This blog post was published November 23, 2016, seventeen days after Donald Trump defeated Hillary Clinton in the presidential election.

Charlottesville, Virginia. We ordered a bottle of Bayten Sauvignon Blanc. It's from the Constantia wine region in South Africa, the oldest wine region in the Southern Hemisphere. It's Cape Town's wine region, at the southern tip of the African continent.

I raised my glass and gently swirled the soft, golden potion, and watched her long legs drift down the glass. Slowly I brought it to my nose and breathed in the granite-born soil where *Homo sapiens* began. I took a long, slow sip, closed my eyes, forgot where I was, and swirled the history of that land in my mouth.

A view from Table Mountain looks out to Robben Island where Nelson Mandela spent the first eighteen of his twenty-seven years in prison. His "Long Walk to Freedom" unlocked the chains for so many. The Boer Wars, gold, diamonds, greed, apartheid, and domination by the powerful came to mind.

Constantia began producing wine in 1685. Fredrick the Great and Napoleon sipped wine produced from the same soil that created what I'm now swirling in my mouth.

Wow, what a sip—now back to reality.

**Cape Town Has Its Granite,
We Have Our Limestone**

Every good wine should engage a sense of place, history, and culture. Today it was Bayten Sauvignon Blanc. Tomorrow it will be from our soil in the Shenandoah Valley.

**President-Elect Trump's Rhetoric
Doesn't Match Reality**

President-elect Trump and his administration do not embrace sustainability and will not lead the world on a path forward for a more holistic and peaceful planet. He pledges to bring back coal, build the Keystone pipeline, eliminate the EPA, and renegotiate NATO while embracing Russian president Vladimir Putin. So far, he has appointed an all-white, male, antiscience, homophobic, bigoted, alt-right inner circle.

The drumbeat to berate public servants and their work has begun. President Ronald Reagan did the same thing in the eighties. I spent eight years fighting his mantra that government workers were lazy, overpaid, and worthless. I stand on my record.

Trump's businesses, led by his children, and his presidency, are fraught with conflicts of interest.

As a public servant for thirty years, I could not accept lunch from a client or a gift over twenty dollars. Our former Virginia governor accepted Rolex watches and catered weddings; he was acquitted of all corruption charges. Trump's businesses linked to his soon-to-be-profound insider knowledge as president are saturated with conflicts of interest. Martha Stewart went to jail for a fraction of that.

Things are not adding up.

A Renewed Environmental Movement Begins

It's time to get back in the game. Your environmental organizations need you more than ever. Volunteer, give money, voice your opinion, run for office, do not give up. Nelson Mandela's "Long Walk to Freedom" took him over twenty-seven years. The Chesapeake Bay Foundation's long walk to restoration has been moving steadily forward for fifty years! We are not letting up now. The Chesapeake Clean Water Blueprint is working. This is not the time to retreat; indeed, it is time to charge forward!

May we have the endurance and grace of Nelson Mandela.

Migrations and Musings

I live in such a beautiful place—it's mostly grasslands and forests. In some places, one cannot see another dwelling in any direction. On most mornings in September, mist hugs the hollows, and heavy dew blankets the ground. Cool nights and shorter days get things in the natural world moving; migrations of many animal species are in full swing.

Swallows and swifts have already flown south, and right now we are in the full swing of raptor migration. The Rockfish Gap hawk-watching station in Afton is one of the best places on the East Coast to experience this phenological phenomenon. We can see Afton from Swoope. It's a gap in the Blue Ridge Mountains on the east flank of the Shenandoah Valley.

The excitement of seeing several hundred Broad-Winged Hawks in one view of your binoculars can never be extinguished. "Oh my God!" is heard often on the mountain as the raptors rise through a thermal in a formation known as a kettle. Once at the top of the thermal, they glide south without wingbeat into the unknown. I was there on September 17, 2017, when over seven thousand Broad-Winged Hawks soared past.

Broad-Winged Hawks nest throughout the Eastern United States and as far north as Canada during the summer and migrate south to Central and South America beginning in late August.

The peak of their migration in Virginia is about the third week in September.

Warblers

All the warblers are in migration. It's a special treat when any warbler stops by to rest and refuel, right in the backyard. I was lucky to spot a group of about six Palm Warblers in the gardens and yard. They nest in Canada's boreal forests during the summer and migrate to the Gulf Coast and the Caribbean for the winter.

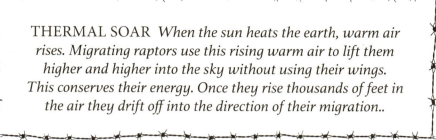

THERMAL SOAR *When the sun heats the earth, warm air rises. Migrating raptors use this rising warm air to lift them higher and higher into the sky without using their wings. This conserves their energy. Once they rise thousands of feet in the air they drift off into the direction of their migration..*

Buckeyes Migrate Too!

Yellow Wingstem is a great pollinator plant. Buckeye Butterflies seek out its nectar before migrating south.

Musings in Swoope

Jeanne is obsessed with removing invasive weeds on the farm. She keeps a corn knife beside her seat in the farm Jeep, and while checking the cows, she will drive to any remaining thistle and whack it down. If she spots a Cocklebur, she will drive to it, get out, and pull it up by the root. I've seen the Jeep full of Cocklebur plants many times.

Jeanne and I are very passionate about a lot of things, especially clean water. We support the Chesapeake Clean Water Blueprint and fight against corporate "takings" for profit, for instance the Atlantic Coast Pipeline that will no doubt damage our streams and alter water sources for many.

SECTION II

MY LIFE'S WORK

This is a collection of essays, published articles, blog posts, and journal excerpts relating to my life's work—what I have been passionate about during my careers, first as a soil conservationist for USDA and now as an environmental consultant, freelance writer, and educator.

Some of the material, especially in the published articles, is redundant; however, I think it is important to keep the articles in context with the conflicts at the time they were written and the publications they were written for. Where appropriate, material has been updated to reflect activity since the article was written.

7
Riparian Buffers

Background

My goal with this chapter is to put the most important material I have written about riparian buffers in one place.

Planting trees on the banks of streams and excluding livestock from these areas are perhaps the two most cost-effective practices to improve water quality. Streamside forests are called riparian forest buffers. The word "riparian" comes from the Latin word that means adjacent to water. Buffers are narrow strips of land that lessen the impact of adjacent upland land uses.

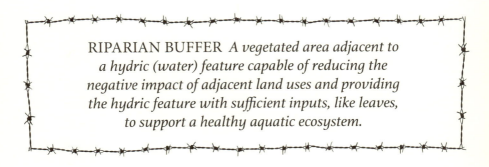

RIPARIAN BUFFER *A vegetated area adjacent to a hydric (water) feature capable of reducing the negative impact of adjacent land uses and providing the hydric feature with sufficient inputs, like leaves, to support a healthy aquatic ecosystem.*

There are two kinds of water pollution: point source and nonpoint source. Point source water pollution comes from any source, such as a pipe, that one could point to and say, "There it is," for example, a discharge pipe from a wastewater treatment plant. Nonpoint source water pollution comes from land that is not adequately cared for. The Environmental Protection Agency (EPA) defines it as any pollution not meeting the definition of point source water pollution. How's that for a bureaucratic definition?

To be fair, nonpoint source water pollution is a bit more difficult to define. It comes from water flowing across large areas such as a landscape, parking lot, or crop field that has pollution-causing agents such as a crop field that has no vegetation on it. Maybe the farmer just plowed and disced the field, leaving it bare and vulnerable to the forces of erosion. When it rains, water flows across the field, picking up particles of soil as it moves downslope toward a ditch or stream. Soil suspended in that runoff water is called sediment and is a pollutant. Same thing happens when water flows across parking lots, feed lots, overfertilized lawns, and so on.

Nonpoint source pollution can also come from lands that are saturated with nutrients such as nitrogen and phosphorus. These lands are usually in areas where farms produce more manure than the surrounding lands can handle. Decades of applying manure on the same farm fields will supersaturate the soils with nitrogen and phosphorus. When this occurs, those nutrients leach into the groundwater and emerge as low-flow, pollutant-laden water in our streams.

I learned about riparian buffers and effective buffer widths when I worked for the Natural Resources Conservation Service, but I did not know how important leaves from native trees were to the aquatic ecosystem until I heard Dr. Bern Sweeney talk about his research at the Stroud Water Research Center in Avondale, Pennsylvania.

Dr. Sweeney's passion is the study of macroinvertebrates and fresh water ecology. The word Macroinvertebrates in general, refers to aquatic animals lacking a backbone that can be seen with the naked eye. These include insects, various worms, snails, clams, and crayfish. The larval stage of Dragonflies, Caddisflies, Mayflies, Stoneflies, and Crane Flies are all aquatic insects and are macroinvertebrates.

Macroinvertebrates serve many purposes. They clean streams and rivers because they consume algae, leaves, and decaying bacteria, plants, and animals. They are also an important food source for fish and birds.

Aquatic insects are the largest group of macroinvertebrates, and many aquatic insect species are leaf shredders. When a leaf falls into the stream from a nearby tree, certain insects will begin to eat it.

Dr. Sweeney's research proves that macroinvertebrates can tell the various species of leaves apart and are often "leaf specific." In other words, Mayfly A may prefer and grow best by eating Red Maple leaves while Mayfly B may prefer and grow best by eating White Oak leaves. This is why scientists recommend planting a diversity of native trees in riparian buffers—to provide a wide diversity of food (leaf types) for the aquatic ecosystem.

Our farm is in the Middle River watershed, near the beginning of the South Fork of the Shenandoah River. I believe that if we had well-functioning riparian buffers along all the streams in our watershed, we could remove our river from the state's Impaired Waters List and return Virginia's state fish, the Brook Trout, to its waters.

Farmers have been installing riparian buffers for many years, and that is partly why agriculture is halfway toward achieving its nutrient reduction goals in the Chesapeake Clean Water Blueprint. Farmers have made this progress through voluntary programs like the Conservation Reserve Program and each state's Best Management Practices program. These programs are funded

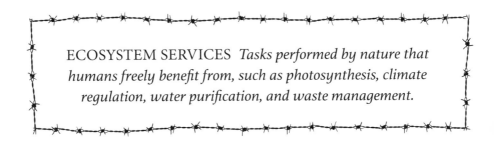

ECOSYSTEM SERVICES *Tasks performed by nature that humans freely benefit from, such as photosynthesis, climate regulation, water purification, and waste management.*

through the U.S. Farm Bill, the EPA, the state, and nonprofit organizations like the Chesapeake Bay Foundation and the Alliance for the Chesapeake Bay.

Riparian buffers provide many ecosystem services, such as filtering runoff water; taking up nutrients; shading the stream, which lowers its temperature; and providing food for the aquatic ecosystem. Scientists believe the minimum width of these buffers needs to be somewhere between thirty-five and one hundred feet on both sides of the stream or hydric feature. The buffer also needs to be stocked with native trees in a sufficient density to create canopy closure—that's when the branches of one tree overlap the branches of another. Livestock must be excluded from the buffer area.

Brook Trout—Our Environmental Refugees

This op-ed was distributed by the Bay Journal News Service on November 10, 2015.

Middle River flows through our farm. Brook Trout, Virginia's state fish, used to thrive in it. They migrated elsewhere—environmental refugees from the sediment-laden waters of the river. The river is slowly being restored, and one day, we will reintroduce this native fish to the waters that flow through our farm.

I walk to the river's edge on our farm and look down at the water. Today its color is milk-chocolate brown—brown from all the sediment and cow manure from upstream farms. The water and everything in it, including sediment, nutrients, and pathogens, is on its way to the Chesapeake Bay.

Middle River is the largest tributary of the South Fork of the Shenandoah River. The South Fork flows north on the east side of Massanutten Mountain. The North Fork flows north on the west side of Massanutten Mountain. The two forks come together at Front Royal to form the Shenandoah River, which joins the Potomac River at Harpers Ferry, West Virginia. The Potomac then flows through our nation's capital on its way to the Chesapeake Bay.

Brook Trout are pollution-sensitive fish. They must have cold and clear water to thrive and survive. I believe they vanished from the river when our ancestors harvested the trees along the riverbanks in the early 1800s. They harvested the trees for many reasons but mainly to clear land to grow crops. Without the trees to shade the water, its temperature rose above the tolerance level for the trout. Also without leaves from native trees, the aquatic ecosystem was devoid of its food source.

But perhaps the biggest culprit in the demise of the fish was soil erosion from the cropland that produced wheat from the end of the American Revolution to the Great Depression. The Great Valley of Virginia was known as the Breadbasket of the Confederacy and produced more wheat than anywhere in the United States. Wheat production at that time involved much soil disturbance such as plowing and discing, which made the land vulnerable to soil erosion.

The sediment from that erosion basically suffocated all the critters that made up healthy aquatic ecosystems. Brook Trout and other pollution-sensitive fish migrated elsewhere to survive (hence the term environmental refugees,) died or because they had nothing to eat.

Today the Shenandoah Valley remains Virginia's largest agricultural region but not for wheat production. The Valley produces more beef cattle than any region in Virginia and perhaps the entire Chesapeake Bay watershed. Cows eat grass, and we can grow a lot of it—this is a good thing. Unfortunately, most of the cattle in our watershed have direct access to streams. They trample the banks and the stream bottoms, thus dislodging soil and destroying aquatic ecosystems. They defecate and urinate in streams, thus polluting the water. Nutrients in manure are one of the main reasons for dead zones in the Chesapeake Bay. Manure also has pathogens in it such as *E. coli*, a bacterium found in the intestines of mammals.

Our river is on Virginia's Impaired Waters List because of sediment and high concentrations of *E. coli*. The state conducted research to determine the source of the bacteria. According to their findings, ninety-four percent of the *E. coli* in our river comes from livestock.

The state standard for *E. coli* in Virginia for freshwater streams is 235 colony forming units per 100 milliliters (cfu/100 mL) of water. Health officials warn that *E. coli* counts above this limit will cause human health problems, and they recommend avoiding "direct contact" with water exceeding this limit. When the river enters our farm, the *E. coli* counts are consistently over 1,000 cfu/100 mL. Whoa, 1,000 cfu! The river flows for one-half mile through our farm with riparian buffers we planted in 2004. When the river exits our farm the *E. coli* count drops, on average, by fifty-five percent.

We fenced the cows out of our part of the river in 2004. Most of the denuded banks are now fully vegetated with native plants, shrubs, and trees. The leaves falling into the river replenish the aquatic ecosystem with the food it needs to restore itself. I call these leaves the corn silage of the aquatic ecosystem.

The *E. coli* count in the river is reduced on our farm partly because the aquatic ecosystems are processing the in-stream pollutants. Science tells us that a stream flowing through a forested buffer is two to eight times more capable of processing in-stream pollutants than a stream without trees along the banks.

I look forward to the day when our entire river is lined with native trees and the cattle are fenced out. When these two practices are implemented, the water will be clear and cold, and once again Brook Trout will thrive.

Trees Remove *E. Coli* Pollution from Streams

The Bay Journal News Service distributed this op-ed on March 7, 2017. USA Today published it on March 17 as "Want a cleaner river? Keep cow pies out, plant trees." E. coli data has been updated to reflect sampling through October 2017.

One of the most polluted rivers in Virginia flows through our farm in the Shenandoah Valley. However, we are witnessing the river's amazing potential to heal. By taking steps like fencing cattle out of streams and planting trees along the banks, *E. coli* bacteria levels can drop.

For over twenty years, the Middle River has been on Virginia's "dirty waters list" because it exceeds the state standard for *E. coli*. It also violates the state's General Standard, meaning there is so much sediment in the water, the river cannot support a healthy aquatic ecosystem.

There is hope for turning that around.

When the river enters our farm, the average *E. coli* level is consistently over 1,000 colony-forming units per one hundred milliliters of water (cfu/100 mL). In October of 2016 it was 6,700. That is more than twenty-eight times Virginia's standard for *E. coli*, which is 235 cfu/100 mL.

But a remarkable thing happens over the course of the farm's half-mile stretch of river. By the time the river leaves our property, the average *E. coli* level drops on average by fifty-five percent.

While that's still pretty polluted, it is a huge improvement. What's happening?

Here's the story.

The river begins just six miles upstream from our farm. By the time it enters our farm, it's nineteen feet across, far too wide to jump. When the weather is cold, the water is crystal clear. But when it's warm out, it looks like chocolate milk.

The cause of the pollution is obvious. Cattle cool off in waterways upstream, where they wallow, defecate, urinate, and tramp up and down streambanks.

The manure that livestock deposit in the river is basically fecal coliform bacteria and nutrients. This devastating contamination can cause livestock and human illnesses and fuel harmful algae blooms. Years ago, the Virginia Department of Conservation and Recreation (DCR) held a meeting with the landowners in our community to inform us that the river was polluted. They told us that most of the pollution was caused by livestock having access to the river and its tributaries.

"It's not us," many said. "You will have to prove it."

So the DCR folks set out to prove it. They worked with a private company and James Madison University (JMU) to track down the sources of the bacteria. They collected water samples from the river and feces from the land, grew cultures from each to see whose bacteria from the land matched up to the bacteria in the water. From its research, JMU concluded that ninetey-four percent of the fecal matter in our river came from livestock. It was proven with empirical data, not a model.

On our farm, we fenced cattle out of the river in 2004 and planted native trees and shrubs along the banks. Many of those trees are now over fifteen feet tall. It's a joy to walk in the shade along the river and see beautiful native flowers such as Jewelweed, Goldenrod, Bur Marigold, and Grand Lobelia. These trees and shrubs do so much for the river. They shade the water, stabilize the streambanks, and provide food and habitat for wildlife.

There are several reasons for the pollution reduction in our meager half mile of the river. Some dilution occurs from groundwater entering the stream. Sunlight kills some of the fecal coliform. But the biggest factor is that we don't have any cows in the river. The second biggest factor is the riparian forest buffer. Leaves from the trees and shrubs help the aquatic ecosystem function by processing pollution.

Here's the research. Scientists from the Stroud Water Research Center in Pennsylvania determined that a stream flowing through forested buffers is two to eight times more capable of processing in stream nitrogen pollution than a stream without trees and shrubs along its banks. That's because leaves from native trees fall into the water and provide food for multitudes of critters that thrive in the water.

Fencing livestock out of streams is beneficial for farmers and for everyone downstream. It can be eight times more beneficial if trees are planted along the streams as well.

If we can get a fifty-five percent reduction in *E. coli* in half a mile, think what a mile, five miles, a hundred miles could do. We have not yet fully recognized the great power of a healthy aquatic ecosystem when it comes to processing and preventing in-stream pollution. It doesn't matter if that pollution comes from a wastewater treatment plant, a malfunctioning septic field, or the back end of a cow.

The bottom line is we can reduce a lot of pollution if we just plant more trees along streams.

 ## Fish Need Leaves

Virginia Wildlife published this article in its January/February 2015 issue.

The sun set half an hour ago. The air thickens with moisture as fog slowly moves in over the river on its unceasing journey. The water riffling over the rocks is all I can hear. It takes me a few minutes to focus on the insects—there must be a hundred of them spinning up and down over the water. These are male Mayflies hovering to mate with females as they fly through the swarm. When Mayflies are present it's a good sign there will be fish. Fish, especially trout, like to eat Mayflies.

Anglers know well the importance of Mayflies, Caddisflies, Stoneflies, Crane Flies, and other insects that spend most of their life in the water. Together, these are called aquatic macroinvertebrates, which means they are large enough to be seen with the naked eye and lack backbones. These insects are also good indicators of clean water, which is necessary for many fish, especially Virginia's native Brook Trout.

The larval stages of these insects are a main food source for many species of fish. From the time the egg hatches through pupation, these insects spend most of their time eating leaves that have fallen into the stream. Scientists call these leaf-eating species "shredders" because they shred and consume fallen leaves; they are the leaf digesters of the streams. When they have grown to full size they will undergo metamorphosis to the winged stage. At this point they move to the surface of the water and take flight. This is called a hatch.

Anglers take great pride in "tying flies" that mimic the insects they think the fish are eating. For example, Quill Gordon and March Brown Flies mimic the Mayflies in the *Heptageniidae* family. These Mayflies are known as "clingers" because of their ability to cling to rocks in fast moving water.

Scientists at the Stroud Water Research Center in Avondale, Pennsylvania, have been studying freshwater ecosystems since the 1960s. Dr. Bernard Sweeney is the director and senior research scientist at Stroud. "A streamside forest along headwater streams is the single most important component for a healthy aquatic ecosystem," he emphasized.

Leaves from streamside forests are the main food sources for macroinvertebrates. It's the bottom of the food chain for trout and other fish. No leaves, no insects, no fish. Not only do trees supply food for the insects, they also provide shade, which keeps the water temperature cool and prevents intense direct sunlight, as opposed to dappled sunlight, from reaching the stream. Thus, the three most important factors in a healthy aquatic ecosystem are food, temperature, and light.

Food

"Even within a group of aquatic insects such as the Mayflies and Crane Flies, species who eat leaves do so preferentially, clearly eating one species of leaf over another when given a choice, perhaps in recognition of the fact that each leaf species has different nutrient values," explained Sweeney.

Researchers at Stroud constructed both indoor and outdoor flumes or artificial stream beds, to test which leaf species each type of aquatic insect preferred.

Sweeney stressed that because each aquatic insect species prefers certain leaf types over others and grows and survives differently on them as well, it is imperative to have a diversity of native trees along streams. An abundance of native trees along a stream supplies an abundance of food for the insects, which will attract and nurture fish.

Temperature

"Each macroinvertebrate species has an optimum temperature regime. One species of Mayfly we studied flourished at sixty-eight degrees but perished at seventy. Keeping water temperatures cool is absolutely critical for these insects. They live on the edge because just a few degrees warmer may be lethal," the scientist insisted.

Trout need cool temperatures as well. Brook Trout thrive when water temperatures are in the sixties. They struggle and often perish when water temperatures are in the seventies or higher.

Trees along streams help keep water temperatures cooler by providing shade during the warmer months. According to Sweeney, on average, forested sections of streams receive seventeen percent less radiation than nonforested streams.

Light

Sweeney and other scientists at Stroud proved that light intensity affects the algae types that grow in a stream. "Algal photosynthesis is a linear function of light intensity," he states in one research paper. In other words, the more light, the more algae. He further suggests that for trout and macroinvertebrates, long filamentous algae (multiple celled), which favors intense light, does not make good habitat. Having plenty of trees along the stream will prevent intense light from reaching the water, thus favoring single cell algae such as diatoms—the algae preferred by macroinvertebrates found in cleaner streams.

Water Quality

Dr. Tom Benzing is a professor of integrated science and technology at James Madison University and vice president for conservation on the Virginia State Council of Trout Unlimited. "To bring back native Brook Trout," he says, "we must improve water quality and restore habitat. Eliminating sediment sources in the water and planting native trees along streams will help trout and the entire aquatic ecosystem."

Sediment sources come from soil that is not protected from the forces of erosion. Exposed soil easily erodes from bare ground, construction sites, denuded ditches, and poorly managed farms. Livestock, especially cattle, devastate fish habitat when they are allowed unlimited access to streams. They not only pollute the water with manure and urine, they trample the stream banks, cause soil erosion, and prevent trees from growing along the banks.

Paul Bugas, aquatics manager with the Virginia Department of Game and Inland Fisheries, stresses this point. "Soil particles clog the gills of fish and smother populations of macroinvertebrates and fish eggs," he says. "Suspended soil particles create cloudy conditions resulting in ecological damage. Unlimited access of cattle in streams absolutely destroys aquatic habitat."

Brook Trout need very clean water, as do Mayflies. "You bring back the Mayflies you will bring back native trout," Benzing says.

To achieve this, we must plant native trees along the banks of our streams, prevent soil from washing off the land, and keep livestock out of the water. Virginia has a plan to bring back the Mayflies and trout; it's called the Watershed Improvement Plan. It calls for planting 103,552 acres of new streamside forests by 2025.

Virginia and the United States Department of Agriculture have programs to help landowners install streamside forests, reduce soil erosion, and fence livestock out of streams. These programs reimburse landowners for the cost of planting trees, planting cover crops, healing eroded areas, installing fences, and livestock watering systems at rates ranging from 75 percent to 140 percent. One program, the Conservation Reserve Enhancement Program, also pays rent on the land that is excluded from livestock, sometimes as much as one hundred dollars per acre per year. Help us achieve this goal by planting native trees along the streams on your property and encourage others to help as well.

To find out how you can help plant more streamside forests, protect soil from eroding, and exclude livestock from streams, contact your local Soil and Water Conservation District, USDA, or the Virginia Department of Forestry office.

By working together, we can bring back both healthy aquatic ecosystems and Virginia's native fish—Brook Trout.

 ## Poague Run: Restoring Trout, Restoring Hope

Virginia Wildlife published this article in its March/April 2016 issue.

Staunton, Virginia. I watched the children carry their jars with native Brook Trout fingerlings to the edge of the stream. They were all smiles as parents gleefully watched a few steps away. The children carefully stepped close to the clear, flowing water, and tipped the jars over, releasing their fish into the stream.

Poague Run was once laden with sediment, sewage, and manure, but now, thanks to the people who live in the watershed and what they did to their land, the stream is clean enough and cold enough for Virginia's native fish to thrive.

Brook Trout are pollution-sensitive fish and must have clean, clear, cold water to flourish.

This successful restoration project is a sterling example of leadership, partnerships, and people working together with nature to turn what was once a quagmire of sediment and sewage-laden waters into a pristine native trout stream.

The restoration journey for Poague Run began in the mid-nineties when Virginia Department of Game and Inland Fisheries biologist Paul Bugas informed the Headwaters Soil and Water Conservation District (SWCD) and the USDA Natural Resources Conservation Service (NRCS) that Poague Run had the water flow and fish structure to support Brook Trout if these organizations could find ways to reduce the pollution.

To understand what was causing the pollution, conservationists delineated the watershed of Poague Run on a map to help them determine the sources for the sediment, sewage, and manure problems.

The Poague Run watershed begins near Staunton's water filtration plant on Shutterlee Mill Road. It includes 2,858 acres of land and is about six miles long. It enters Lewis Creek just east of Interstate 81 at exit 225.

Beginning at the very top of the watershed, or at the highest elevation within the watershed, there is no flowing stream; it's just land that slopes toward the stream. Eventually, springs gurgle up out of the ground here and there. It's like the capillaries in our vascular system. Several join up, and eventually they make a vein or, in this case, a small stream. One small stream joins another to form a larger stream. And so on, downstream.

Poague Run has sixteen small streams that flow into it. These tributaries don't have names. Poague Run joins Lewis Creek, Lewis Creek joins the Middle River, the Middle River joins other rivers to form the South Fork of the Shenandoah River, the Shenandoah joins the Potomac, and the Potomac enters the Chesapeake Bay.

Sediment and Manure Suffocate Aquatic Habitat

Sediment is one of the leading causes of water pollution and is deadly to the kinds of critters that Brook Trout feed on. Virginia's native trout feed on aquatic insects like Mayflies, Stoneflies, and Caddisflies, all of which have external gills. As I have said before, when sediment is in the water, it clogs the gills of these insects and suffocates them.

Most of the sediment issues in Poague Run were from cattle lounging in the stream. Cattle trample the stream banks dislodging soil. They also trample the streambed, stirring up sediment.

Cattle also pollute the stream with manure and urine. Manure contains nutrients and pathogens that negatively affect the aquatic ecosystem.

If the landowners in Poague Run wanted Brook Trout in their stream, the cows would have to be fenced out.

Sewage Pollutes Water

About sixty percent of the watershed is urban, with many houses, streets, and a few businesses. There were leaking sewer pipes and a few septic system failures.

The Water Is Cold

Dr. Tom Benzing obtained a grant to install water temperature sensors in the stream to determine whether the water was cold enough in the summer to support Brook Trout.

According to Benzing, "The data from three sensors along the mile and a half of perennial flow indicated that the water temperature could in fact support Brook Trout."

The Strategic Plan to Restore the Watershed

The plan included extensive public outreach efforts such as workshops, field days, newsletters, and, most important, seeking input from the people who live in the watershed. Many conservation partners were involved with the restoration process, including the landowners, USDA, the Headwaters SWCD, the Shenandoah Resource Conservation, and Development Council, the Virginia Department of Forestry, Virginia Cooperative Extension, the Virginia Department of Game and Inland Fisheries, Trout Unlimited, the Chesapeake Bay Foundation, Chesapeake Funders Network, Friends of Middle River, and the Valley Conservation Council.

Representatives from these organizations assisted with developing newsletters, obtaining funding to help pay for projects, and building public awareness.

The first agricultural projects began in 1998 when cousins Lewis and John Moore started fencing cows out of the streams on their farms. This was the year USDA began funding livestock stream exclusion and planting native trees along narrow corridors beside streams. These are called riparian forest buffers. These projects were funded through the Conservation Reserve Program.

Lee and Allison Hereford own Merrifield Farm. The perennial flow of Poague Run begins on their farm. They participated in several of the programs.

"The programs helped us install livestock watering stations all over the farm," Lee explains, "so now we can rotate the cows to different pastures. It allows us to better utilize the forage on the farm. We have much fewer disease problems too."

Carolyn Moore Ford, owner of Rolling Hills Farm, also participated. "I like to fly-fish, and I thought how wonderful it would be if I could do that on my farm," Ford said. "I fenced the cows out of the stream, and it was amazing how fast the stream banks healed, and now the water runs so clear."

The City and Headwaters SWCD Team Up to Fix the Sewage Problems

The Headwaters SWCD obtained a grant from the Virginia Department of Conservation and Recreation (DCR) to assist landowners with correcting malfunctioning septic systems. Sandy Greene administered the grant for Headwaters. "Once we advertised that we had funds to help with septic problems," she explains, "the money was obligated within two weeks."

The city of Staunton helped with sewer hookups. The city also installed a sewage lift station to handle more sewer connections.

It's All Done

Many conservation treatments have been installed on the land, making the water in Poague Run clear, clean, and cold.

Landowners and farmers have excluded livestock from 5.8 miles of stream banks, established forty-four acres of riparian buffers, planted over six thousand trees and shrubs, and established twenty-five acres of early successional habitat for Northern Bobwhites and other grassland birds. Three houses were hooked up to the city's sewage system, and all malfunctioning septic systems were fixed either by septic pump-outs or by installing new systems.

The People and the City Celebrate

Restoring the watershed and hence the stream started in 1998 and was completed in 2014. On a beautiful sunny day in April 2014, hundreds of people came out to Rolling Hills Farm to help celebrate working farms, conservation, and clean streams; it was the inaugural "Kites and Critters" field day sponsored by the Valley Conservation Council, a private land trust serving the Shenandoah Valley region.

Now the city of Staunton and the people living in the Poague Run watershed can boast of a clean stream, working farms, and native trout. Congratulations to the landowners and farmers in the Poague Run watershed and to all the people that made this happen.

Everyone benefits from good land use. What happened in Poague Run is going on in small watersheds all over Virginia and throughout the Chesapeake Bay watershed, and it can occur in the watershed where you live.

What is the status of the watershed where you live?

The following are other essays on riparian buffers.

Cattle Destroy Streams

Livestock that have access to streams and rivers pollute the water with their manure and urine. But perhaps even worse, when they access a stream and hang out to cool off, their hooves gouge and disturb the bottom habitat making it unsuitable for many aquatic plants and animals. Their sharp hooves also gouge and dislodge soil from the banks of the stream, which then chokes and kills aquatic life.

On average, a mature cow weighs half a ton. Think about a herd of fifty half-ton cows with hooves like big ice cream scoops climbing up and down a stream bank. The soil their hooves rip out gets in the stream. If cows are in the stream, the water is going to be brown, like chocolate milk, because of all the dislodged soil suspended in the water.

Dislodged soil that enters the water smothers and suffocates the aquatic ecosystem. For example, the larval stages of Mayflies,

Dragonflies, and Stoneflies have external gills. Sediment in the water clogs those gills causing suffocation and death.

I stood on the bank of Middle River looking downstream at a farm that allows cattle into the river. All the stream banks were denuded of vegetation.

I turned around, on the same spot, and looked upstream. The farmer of this land removed his cattle from the river in 2002. The banks of the river are covered with vegetation. Little if any soil is exposed.

Fencing livestock, especially cattle, out of streams and rivers is vital for functioning aquatic ecosystems, cleaner streams, and a restored Chesapeake Bay. The practice offers many advantages for farmers as well, such as healthier livestock, ease of herd movement, and the elimination of calving risk areas.

Why Do Farmers Fence Livestock Out of Streams?

Why do farmers fence their livestock from ponds, streams, and wetlands? Of the hundreds of farmers I have talked to who have done so, these are the top four reasons:

1. To facilitate better water distribution across the entire farm.
2. To improve herd health and reduce biosecurity risks.
3. To eliminate calving risk areas.
4. To facilitate rotational grazing and ease of livestock movement.

Here are the top reasons they don't participate in government programs to exclude livestock from streams:

1. Fear of government intrusion.
2. They don't trust the government.
3. Too much red tape.
4. They don't feel they are causing a problem.

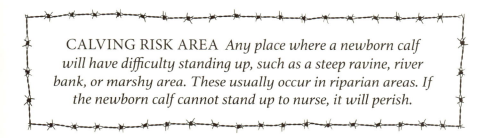

CALVING RISK AREA *Any place where a newborn calf will have difficulty standing up, such as a steep ravine, river bank, or marshy area. These usually occur in riparian areas. If the newborn calf cannot stand up to nurse, it will perish.*

A healthier environment or a restored Chesapeake Bay are not high on the priority list for some farmers. But saving a calf from freezing to death in a wetland or from severe diarrhea are high on their list.

Folks attempting to convince farmers to fence their livestock out of streams need to keep the farmers' goals in mind. To sell this best management practice to farmers, it is important to showcase how the practice will benefit the farmer first, and then the environment.

Testimonials from respected farmers also help. One of the most respected cattle producers and large animal veterinarians in the Shenandoah Valley is Dr. John Wise. He looks a lot like John Wayne: tall, barrel chested, always wearing a cowboy hat and leather vest. He's got a deep voice too. He is one of the founders of Westwood Animal Hospital west of Staunton, Virginia.

Dr. Wise informs us: "Abundant clean water is essential for the health of cattle. Leptospirosis, *E. coli*, and mastitis are the main health problems with cattle drinking dirty water.

"Streams and the river on our home place were especially dangerous during calving, so we fenced them off too. Before that I recall pulling a calf out of Middle River almost every year, many of them dead," he said.

Dr. Wise has participated in many programs to help address these livestock issues. The benefits to the farmer of having abundant clean water and stream exclusion include better weight gains, lower vet bills, healthier livestock, better use of forage, lower mortality, and ease of herd movement. These are farmer benefits that sell conservation too.

Planting and Growing a Successful Riparian Forest Buffer

I have been involved with over six hundred miles of riparian buffer plantings and have witnessed plenty of failures and successes. I would like to share with you what I believe is the recipe for success in achieving canopy closure in ten years.

I'll get right to the point, and then provide details.
- First, and most important, you have to plant the right tree the right way in the right place.
- Second, you must control invasive weeds that are harmful to your seedling.
- Finally, you must maintain your tree shelters.

If you do these three simple things, I believe you will achieve seventy percent tree canopy closure in ten years.

Now for the details. In the Chesapeake Bay watershed, we know from science that forested buffers are extremely effective at filtering out pollutants before they reach the stream. They supply the inputs to the stream that support a healthy aquatic ecosystem. A stream with forested buffers is two to eight times more capable of detoxifying itself than one without streamside forests.

The drivers of the aquatic ecosystem are leaves from native trees; they're the energy source, or bottom, of the aquatic food chain. No leaves, no macroinvertebrates, no fish. The critters in the aquatic ecosystem consume or process pollutants such as fecal bacteria and nutrients.

By planting native hardwoods along a stream, we help Mother Nature establish a forest in ten years instead of thirty to fifty years. Let's look at what we are up against. In pasture, hay land, or meadow, we are inserting a two-to-three-year-old seedling into a sea of mature grassroots. One of the most prevalent grasses in the Bay watershed is Tall Fescue, and we know that it is allelopathic toward tree seedlings. Unmowed grassland is also great habitat for meadow voles—one of a baby tree's worst enemies. Rabbits and deer will also harm the seedlings.

Suppressing Tall Fescue helps your seedling by reducing competition for nutrients and water, removing toxins in the soil, and reducing vole habitat.

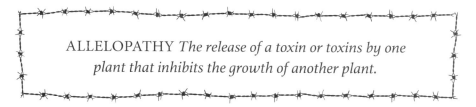

ALLELOPATHY *The release of a toxin or toxins by one plant that inhibits the growth of another plant.*

What Causes Tree Seedling Failure?

There are many reasons for tree seedling failure.

1. No tree shelter. Science tells us that tree shelters are a must. Without shelters, expect seventy percent mortality. With properly installed shelters expect only ten to thirty percent mortality.
2. Improperly installed tree shelter. Shelters need to be in the ground two to three inches below the soil surface. This prevents voles and mice from entering the shelter and killing the seedling.

3. A broken tree shelter stake. When the tree shelter stake breaks, it leaves an opening for voles. Use only White Oak stakes or pressure-treated stakes. Replace broken stakes as soon as possible.
4. Inferior seedling or wrong tree species for the site. Tree seedlings need to be at least a quarter of an inch in diameter at the collar or eighteen inches tall. Select the right tree for the soil type; for instance, don't plant a White Oak in poorly drained soil.

I already mentioned the toxicity of Tall Fescue to tree seedlings. It is important to suppress fescue in some way. A vigorous scalping of the sod prior to planting, use of a turf mat, herbicide treatment, tillage, or some other method can do this.

Other invasive weeds can choke out the seedling as well, and it is important to keep them in check. These include Japanese Hops, Carpetweed, and Field Bindweed. These vines smother seedlings.

I believe we should also suppress invasive weeds that are unacceptable to the community, not only because they give the buffer programs a bad image but because they also prevent the native plants from thriving and building up an appropriate habitat. Such invasives include nonnative thistles, Teasel, Autumn Olive, and others. Be a good neighbor, and keep these weeds under control. A well-managed buffer will convince others that they, too, want to plant buffers on their land.

Riparian forest buffers are key to a restored stream in your community and to a restored Chesapeake Bay—the largest estuary in America.

Riparian Buffer Management—
Control Invasives, Encourage Natives

As summer moves closer to autumn, it seems we have more native plants in the various riparian buffers around the farm. Butterfly Weed, Jewelweed, Wingstem, Purpletop, and many other plants are in bloom now. But many invasive, nonnative plants are in bloom as well.

I have written many times about the importance and benefits of excluding livestock from riparian areas. But we cannot exclude livestock from these areas and just walk away. Management of riparian buffers is vital not only for the quality of wildlife habitat but for the acceptance of this practice in the community. Tree shelter maintenance, vole control, and invasive species control are all vital management strategies for a successful riparian buffer. This essay is about invasive plant control and highlights some of the native plants thriving in our riparian buffers.

Nothing un-sells riparian buffer programs quicker than an area full of invasive species. Quite frankly, it turns farmers off. We must do a better job of managing riparian areas.

We fight invasives year-round. Musk Thistle, Canada Thistle, Bull Thistle, Carpetweed, Teasel, and Cocklebur are the main ones that sneak into our riparian buffers here in Swoope, but we have many others, including Tall Fescue, Autumn Olive, Japanese Knotweed, Japanese Hops, Multiflora Rose, Creeping Charlie, Prickly Lettuce, Bradford Pear, Tree of Heaven, and Wineberry. We use hoes, mowers, herbicides, and hand pulling as necessary to suppress their growth.

Jeanne and I spent a couple of hours the other day in one of her mother's fields, where we had fenced the cows out of a pond and wetland. Our job was to cut the seed heads off of Bull Thistles and then cut the plant down. It was too late to use an herbicide; that's why we were cutting the seed heads off. We cut the seed heads off the plant to prevent the seeds from reproducing. After we cut them off we put them in a container and transported everything to a burn pile.

Bull Thistles have very long thorns that will readily go through leather gloves; we each had to wear two pairs of gloves to complete our tasks.

Bull Thistle is a biennial native to Europe, Western Asia, and Northeastern Africa. Hard to believe, but it's the national flower of Scotland. Although the plant is not native here and is invasive, American Goldfinches eat the seeds and use the downy attachment of the seed for nesting material. Butterflies, moths, and flies seek its nectar and pollen. But it does spread quickly, taking the space other more beneficial plants could have, and it's offensive to farmers because it's a weed. So we take it out.

As we worked, I was amazed at all the native plants and pollinators. This particular riparian area was full of Butterfly Weed, which attracts many pollinators. It's in the milkweed family.

Another native plant in bloom in late summer is Purpletop. This perennial warm-season grass is also known as grease grass because the seeds are oily.

Riparian areas are also great places to let Common Milkweed prosper. We trim a portion of milkweed in July so it will resprout with tender leaves. Monarchs are more attracted to the tender leaves than the older, tougher leaves.

Riparian buffers help improve water quality in our streams and wetlands. These buffers are vital for restoring stream health and the Chesapeake Bay. They are also the best landscapes for wildlife because they provide food, shelter, and water. To be successful, though, we must control invasive species and let native plants prosper.

American Sycamore: Fortress of the Stream Bank

One of eastern North America's greatest native trees is the American Sycamore. Perhaps the most endearing feature of this legendary tree is its bark, especially in winter when the white bark, mottled with green and brown, is fully exposed.

These trees often exceed one hundred feet tall and stand guard along streams like the bones of giant wizards, protecting the banks from erosion and providing many ecosystem services.

Sycamores are one of the most important riparian trees because they readily colonize deforested areas: their seeds are spread by wind and water. They grow fast, and cuttings will easily take root. I have seen poles that were cut from living sycamore branches and inserted into prepared holes take root and prosper.

According to the late Donald Peattie, botanist, "The Sycamore is, in girth of trunk, the largest deciduous hardwood of North America." In 1802 Francois Michaux measured a sycamore on the banks of the Ohio River "at four feet beyond the surface of the soil, and found it forty-seven feet in circumference. So it was that pioneers often stabled a horse, cow, or hog in a hollow sycamore, and sometimes a whole family took shelter in such a hospitable giant."

The fruiting structures of the sycamore are often called button balls because they are round and about one inch in diameter. When the seed balls mature they split apart, revealing their nutlets with downy awns that resemble dandelion seeds.

The wood is hard and difficult to split. Pioneers used round slices of the trunk as solid wheels, and Native Americans used the hollowed-out trunks for canoes. Today the wood is used to make butcher blocks because of its unwillingness to crack and split.

But trees provide much more than wood. They provide shade that cools the water from its adjoining stream. Leaves feed aquatic insects such as Crane Fly larvae. Roots hold the soil on the banks of the stream and take up nutrients. The leaves have stomata, which sequester carbon; the seeds are food for wildlife.

Trees provide cover for all sorts of critters and beauty for us to admire. These ecosystem services are vital to the improvement of both air and water quality. That's why there is so much emphasis on planting trees beside streams. Forested lands adjacent to water are called riparian forest buffers and there are many programs to assist with installing them.

Happy Fifteenth Birthday to Our Riparian Buffer

The riparian buffers on our farm on Middle River are now fifteen years old. Fifteen years ago, the "River Farm" was basically a cool-season grass pasture with a few scattered mature trees along the banks of the river. Now, in addition to excellent forage for cattle, hundreds of native trees and shrubs and thousands of native plants create diverse wildlife habitats on land that provides food for a thriving aquatic ecosystem.

Fifteen years ago, this forty-acre farm was one big pasture. The Middle River meanders through it for a half mile, and two unnamed, intermittent streams seep out of the ground and flow to the river. It had no internal fences for the pasture, and the cows had access to all the water features including the river.

To move the cows from this big pasture to the barn was a chore fraught with frustration. If the cows didn't want to go to the barn they could cross the river multiple times at any number of their favorite crossings, leaving us on the other side cursing wildly and bewildered because we had no way to cross the ten-foot-wide river unless we went back out to the road—it's a bad day when you are outsmarted by bovines!

The Government Helped Us

In 2004, we enrolled in USDA's Conservation Reserve Program. We have two, fifteen-year contracts: one called CP-29 and the other CP-22.

The CP-29 contract for 2.0 acres, had a minimum average setback from hydric features of twenty feet; ideal for a cattleman who desired more pasture and less buffer. At that time USDA did not require us to plant anything in this narrow buffer as long as we could find four native species in the area we were fencing off.

The CP-22 contract for 3.9 acres, required a minimum setback of 35 feet and 110 hardwood trees per acre. This is the Conservation Reserve Enhancement Program (CREP).

We have 5.9 acres of riparian buffer, a half mile on Middle River and 0.12 miles for each of the two intermittent streams. It was a big project creating two alternative livestock watering stations, three stream crossings, 1.5 miles of fence, and a hardwood tree planting. We used the hydric features and fences to create five smaller fields for rotational grazing.

Now, fifteen years later, we can get the cows to the barn with ease, the cows drink cleaner water, and we can rest in the shade of the riparian trees.

This farm produces not only grass for beef but wildlife and cleaner water as well.

My wife, Jeanne, is a ninth-generation farmer. She knows cattle. I'm an environmentalist, I know soil and water. Together we made this farm into a showcase of how compromise and working together can achieve much more than our individual pursuits. We can indeed farm and improve the environment.

Our two USDA contracts expired on September 30, 2018. We will not renew the contracts because the CP-29 program doesn't exist anymore and Virginia offers a program that pays a dollar per foot of stream exclusion. It's called the Continuing Conservation Initiative and is explained in the Virginia Agricultural BMP Cost-Share Manual.

We have learned so much in this short fifteen-year period. In the CREP area, tree canopy closure was achieved in just seven years. That's because we applied management.

Lessons Learned: Cows

Rotational grazing is good for the cows and the pastures. It's much easier to call cows and lead them than it is to push them to the desired location. In rotational grazing, the grass is greener on the other side, so they naturally want to move there.

An exclusion fence is a significant insurance against calf mortality. Swamps, steep ravines, and streams are dangerous places for cows to have a newborn calf. Calves that cannot get up because the wet muck sucked their legs in or because it's too steep for them to stand up will perish before they can nurse.

Water is often the limiting factor in creating a rotational grazing system.

Lessons Learned: Trees

You can't just plant trees and walk away. You have to plant the right tree in the right place and maintain the tree shelter. Keep Tall Fescue and voles away from the tree seedling.

I wish we had planted more trees and shrubs in the CP-29 area. In the CREP area where we planted native hardwoods according to the Virginia Department of Forestry hardwood tree planting guide at the time, the trees are twenty feet tall, and many have a diameter greater than six inches at breast height. The forest floor in the CREP is totally shaded.

In the CP-29 CREP area, we did not plant trees as we did in the CREP area. We planted trees and shrubs here and there just about every year with some success. The native pioneer trees, however, did much better.

Native trees will come if you let them. Walnut, Green Ash, Sycamore, and Catalpa are the most prolific in our area.

If you plant a tree, you must help it along. Voles and fescue will try to kill it. Tree shelters work, but you must maintain the stakes. Shelters should be removed when the tree can support itself, and you must put some sort of deer deterrent on the tree to prevent deer rubs.

In 2004 we used the Virginia Department of Forestry's Hardwood Tree Planting Guide. We followed it and it worked.

Lessons Learned: Wildlife Habitat

Plant habitat and they will come. Our riparian buffers are so vibrant with wildlife. Willow Flycatchers, Indigo Buntings, Blue Grosbeaks, Warbling Vireos, Monarch Butterflies, and so many more species come to nest and feast in our riparian buffers.

Wildflowers and native grasses include Jewelweed, Boneset, Grand Lobelia, Solidago, Wingstem, Ironweed, Mexican Hat, Maximilian Sunflower, Common Milkweed, Butterfly Weed, Bur Marigold, Switchgrass, Indiangrass, and Big Bluestem.

Lessons Learned: Water Quality

Removing cattle from the streams and river improved water quality. Most of the stream banks healed on their own, and *E. coli* is reduced on average by fifty-five percent. We know this because we sampled the river when it enters the farm and when it leaves the farm a half mile downstream. We sampled the river every month for two years for the Friends of the Middle River. Sample results for all sites are on the Friends' website.

Lessons Learned: Invasive Plants

There will always be invasive plants. They are ephemeral in population; first, it was thistle, then Teasel, now Carpetweed and Bur Cucumber.

Lessons Learned: Program Assistance

There is not enough emphasis by program managers on management in newly planted buffers. A buffer full of invasive weeds and empty tree shelters is a huge detriment to streamside buffer programs.

Well-managed buffers and healthy trees are excellent marketing tools. Local nonprofits and volunteers have had great success in managing newly planted buffers and old ones as well.

Conclusion—Riparian Buffers Work for the Farmer and Our Streams

Riparian buffers, especially riparian forest buffers, are the single most cost-effective best management practice to improve freshwater streams. This, coupled with increased livestock watering stations and internal fencing, can greatly improve grazing distribution, ease of herd movement, and herd health, and it can reduce calf mortality. Riparian buffers are a win-win for the farmer and our streams.

8
Calls for Action

Torpedoes, Trump, and the Clean Water Act at 45

This post became an op-ed piece distributed by the Bay Journal News Service on October 17, 2017. USA Today *published it on October 19, 2017.*

The Clean Water Act is forty-five years old this week, having been born in the U.S. Congress on October 18, 1972. Sometime before this day, the river of my childhood, the Roanoke River in southwestern Virginia, had been declared a fire hazard because of pollution.

I learned to waterski on that river, or rather on one of the man-made lakes along its winding path. I remember one of those skiing lessons in particular. It was 1965. Dad was the spotter, and his friend George was the driver. I jumped in the water and waited for the handles of the ski rope. When the tips of my skis were up and my butt down, I yelled, "Forward!"

As the boat began pulling me forward, I saw banana peels and "floaters"—human waste—drifting past. I was ten years old, and it gave me the heebie-jeebies. "Hit it!" I shouted, doubly motivated to get up and out of the water

Today, America has perhaps the best wastewater treatment in the world. All industries and municipalities that discharge pollution into U.S. waters must have permits to do so. They cannot exceed their allocation of pollution. It's regulation that works. It was not easy getting to this point. There was much gnashing of teeth, whining, and litigation, and many political feuds, but all "point" sources of pollution (those coming out of a pipe) in this country are now regulated. For good reason.

And now we've turned our attention to the far more complex problem of "nonpoint" source water pollution—pollution that finds its way into rivers and streams from virtually everywhere. It comes from stormwater runoff from roads, roofs, parking lots, overfertilized lawns, golf courses, bare ground, crop fields, and overgrazed pastures. This runoff may include pollutants such as soil particles, pesticides, seepage from malfunctioning septic fields, livestock waste, and all sorts of other human and natural activities.

We've come a long way since the passage of the Clean Water Act. Before then, we occasionally worried about industrial pollution, but we never spoke of stormwater management, nutrient management, riparian buffers, livestock exclusion from streams, no-till farming, conservation easements, rain gardens, or any other best management practices that today add up to greatly improved water quality.

Before my first successful waterski on that polluted lake, there was no Chesapeake Bay Foundation (founded 1967). There was no Earth Day (April 22, 1970) or EPA (December 2, 1970), and precious few scientists specialized in studying water quality or the effects of nutrient-choked water on aquatic plants and animals. The terms nonpoint source water pollution, watershed restoration, greenways, and blueways had yet to enter the common vernacular.

The Clean Water Act gave us a roadmap for responsible land use, and today our streams, rivers, lakes, and estuaries are measurably cleaner than they were in the 1960s. This despite the fact that we've added over one hundred million people to the U.S. population.

The Chesapeake Bay watershed alone is home to more than eighteen million people, and that number is expected to hit twenty million by 2030. Given those disadvantages, the progress is pretty impressive.

We've made great strides by using the law, sound science, strong partnerships, outdoor education, advocacy, incentives, consequences for blatant polluters, and litigation, all enabled by the Clean Water Act and driven by people and organizations that believe clean water is good for all.

We are moving forward for cleaner water, and we can celebrate major achievements, such as a freshwater stream once again supporting Brook Trout or a wastewater treatment plant discharging cleaner water than the stream it dumps into. The Chesapeake Bay, America's largest estuary, had no dead zones in 2016—the first time since the 1960s.

Think of all the cities and towns that now have walkways along their rivers or streams because of cleaner water. In Virginia alone, we have Alexandria, Richmond, Strasburg, Lexington, Luray, Waynesboro, and many more. Think of all the jobs created by our desire for cleaner water: nurseries growing trees and shrubs for stream buffers, for example, or contractors hired to build fences to keep cows out of streams. One company, Conservation Services in Waynesboro, Virginia, supplies the entire North American continent with tree shelters.

The benefits of clean water are immeasurable—more recreation, more seafood, healthier livestock, and a stronger economy. As they say, a rising tide lifts all ships.

But there are now torpedoes of ignorance, greed, and science denial in the water, launched by the Trump administration and aimed at the fundamental environmental laws that have gotten us so far. I gnash my teeth. They want to water down the definition of "Waters of the United States" so that polluters can get away with pollution-causing violations and thereby increase their profit margins. They want to zero out funding for the Chesapeake Bay Program and for clean water initiatives everywhere and seek to discredit scientists or hide or destroy their research.

I say damn the torpedoes, full speed ahead. We, every last one of us, need to tell our representatives in Washington that clean water is vital to our future as a country and insist that they continue to fully fund clean water initiatives.

We simply cannot afford to weaken the Clean Water Act; we cannot afford to go back to the filthy water of the 1960s.

Unwise Plan for Pipeline Calls for People Power

This op-ed piece was distributed by the Bay Journal News Service on September 23, 2014. Note that some of the facts and figures, such as cost and length, have changed since this writing.

The tidal wave of corporate greed and power continues to grow. Duke Energy, Dominion Power, and now the governor of Virginia [former governor Terry McAuliffe] are all behind the construction of a five-hundred-fifty-mile, forty-two-inch diameter natural gas pipeline. Called the Atlantic Coast Pipeline, it would run across the Allegheny Mountains, through the Great Valley of Virginia, and then across the Blue Ridge to the Atlantic.

Why? In Dominion's words, "We are wholesalers of gas; we just move gas around." The company wants to move fracked gas from its source in West Virginia to its customers, wherever they might be.

In my opinion, "For export."

It's a five billion dollar project.

The pipeline should not be built. It's dangerous and "the People" don't want it.

The Valley of Virginia is underlain by a geologic formation called karst. Karst terrain is formed when water dissolves the minerals beneath the soil to form sinkholes and caverns. The earth's surface caves in or subsides, forming depressions in the landscape called sinkholes. These cave-ins would leave overlaid sections of the pipeline suspended across chasms underground, sometimes causing them to bend and rupture. It is very difficult to find a route through the Valley of Virginia that does not go through karst terrain.

The route Dominion has chosen goes through Augusta County, the widest part of the karst formation in the Valley. At least thirty known sinkholes exist in the direct path of the proposed pipeline in the county.

According to Virginia's Hazard Mitigation Plan of 2013, "Pipeline infrastructure, underlain by karst terrain, can be damaged by a collapse in the supporting soil."

Augusta County has a high incidence of soil subsidence resulting from this active geologic formation. The Virginia Department of Transportation had to shut down a section of Interstate 81 in Augusta County in 2011 because a sinkhole opened. I've seen sinkholes open up in Augusta County that could swallow an eighteen-wheeler.

According to the U.S. Department of Transportation, 2012 alone saw eighty natural gas pipeline explosions and fires nationwide. Since 2001, natural gas pipeline explosions have caused forty-five deaths.

Have we learned nothing from the San Bruno pipeline explosion near San Francisco in 2010 that wiped a neighborhood off the map? It leveled three dozen houses and killed eight people. The explosion created a seventy-two-foot wide crater and threw a three-thousand-pound section of pipe one hundred feet. This was a thirty-inch pipeline. Dominion proposes to build a forty-two-inch pipe from West Virginia to the Atlantic Ocean.

A natural gas pipeline through this type of active geology is not wise and lacks concern for human life. Dominion should instead put its five billion dollars into solar power or into ways to increase energy efficiencies.

The pipeline would go across the Monongahela and George Washington National Forests, the Blue Ridge Parkway (a national park) and the Appalachian Trail (a national scenic trail). It would be given construction right-of-way up to 125 feet wide through these important protected areas. The aftermath would be a seventy-five-foot permanently cleared easement on which no trees are allowed. That equates to nine acres of lost farm and forest for every mile of pipeline—4,950 acres total.

Blasting would be inevitable because of all the rocks. Dominion has said as much. This means clear-cutting, forest fragmentation, and risk to water resources affecting millions of people.

But the people against the pipeline are even more upset about the erosion of their rights and the devaluation of their property. Dominion has the right to enter our property without our permission and, if the Federal Energy Regulatory Commission approves the pipeline, the company can take property rights through eminent domain. The former was granted under Virginia's Wagner Act in 2004 and the latter under the Commerce Clause of the U.S. Constitution.

It's Robin Hood in reverse. The rich take from the poor to give to themselves. How did corporations accumulate so much power? It's been a long and constant process, beginning perhaps with the railroad boom in the 1880s. Beginning in the 1880s, many court cases provided an incremental but ever-mounting surge of power for corporations.

Citizens United v. Federal Elections Commission removed any limits on corporate political campaign contributions. *Kelo v. City of New London* grants the right of eminent domain "takings" for economic purposes.

Today, it seems corporations have more rights than people. Shouldn't it be the other way around?

 ## Atlantic Coast Pipeline: Mayhem of Construction

The News Leader *of Staunton, Virginia, published an op-ed version of this piece on August 15, 2017.*

Dominion's Atlantic Coast Pipeline (ACP), if allowed to be built, will be the largest disturbance of land and water in the Commonwealth of Virginia since the interstate highways were built. Is it possible or even probable that Dominion can dig up a six-hundred-mile-long, ten-foot-deep, seventy-five-foot-wide swath through three states, crossing hundreds of streams and meet each state's water quality standards? I do not believe it is possible or probable.

The ACP will unearth 9,090 acres (that's about 9,090 football fields) of Virginia, or put another way, 396 million square feet. That's 15.6 times larger than the footprint of the largest office building on the planet—the Pentagon, which covers 583 acres.

The ACP in Virginia will be almost as long as Interstate 81 is in Virginia, which is 325 miles.

Have you ever seen a construction project that did not have brown water leaving the site after a rain? I have not, even with the proper erosion-and-sediment-control practices such as silt fences and catch basins. Runoff from construction sites is brown because soil particles are suspended in it.

State Code of Virginia: *All state waters, including wetlands, are designated for the following uses: recreational uses, e.g., swimming and boating; the propagation and growth of a balanced, indigenous population of aquatic life . . .*

How can any public body or any rational person believe this much earth moving and blasting will not pollute streams, destroy aquatic life, or disrupt the underground water supplies we depend on?

In the Virginia Department of Environmental Quality's (DEQ) own written comments to the Federal Energy Regulatory Commission (FERC) concerning the ACP, it states, "Dye traces within the general project area have shown connections of karst features to springs and wells as far away as 7 miles . . . ."

The ACP's planned mayhem of construction will go through the water recharge area of Gardner Spring, which supplies the city of Staunton, population 24,000, with half its water. The spring's recharge area is in karst geology. How many water recharge areas will the six-hundred-mile mayhem of construction go through? How much aquatic life will this destroy?

The DEQ states that it will study every foot of upland disturbance the ACP creates. It should study, review, and permit every stream and wetland crossing as well. But it is not proposing to do that.

It plans to give this responsibility to the Army Corps of Engineers from which Dominion hopes to receive a "blanket" permit for all stream and wetland crossings. The planned ACP will cross 189 streams and forty-three wetlands in Augusta County alone.

Farmers must get a permit for their cows to cross a stream. Shouldn't Dominion be held to the same standard?

Dominion needs a 401 certification from the Virginia State Water Control Board (SWCB) to build its Atlantic Coast Pipeline. The board has the authority and the responsibility to certify that Dominion's construction of the pipeline will not violate Virginia's water quality standards.

Governor Northam: These Pipelines Aren't Being Done 'Right'

This op-ed was published in the News Leader *on July 12, 2018, and the* Roanoke Times *on July 19, 2018.*

"If we are going to do this, we are going to do it right," Dr. Ralph Northam said on the campaign trail to become governor of Virginia, referring to the Mountain Valley Pipeline (MVP) and Atlantic Coast

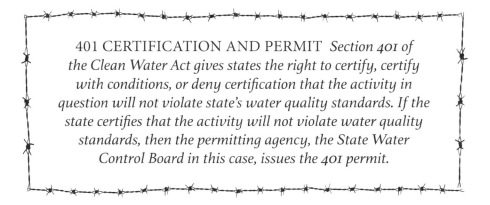

401 CERTIFICATION AND PERMIT *Section 401 of the Clean Water Act gives states the right to certify, certify with conditions, or deny certification that the activity in question will not violate state's water quality standards. If the state certifies that the activity will not violate water quality standards, then the permitting agency, the State Water Control Board in this case, issues the 401 permit.*

Pipeline (ACP), two forty-two-inch-diameter gas pipelines planned to be built across Virginia's Allegheny and Blue Ridge Mountains.

Governor Northam, it's not being done right, and without the right steps forward from your administration, Virginia's water resources and everyone in the path of these projects will remain at risk.

I hear from the opposite side that these pipelines have been through the most rigorous environmental review process in history. If that is true, then we have a flawed system. The courts have revoked various permits; more lawsuits have been filed than I can count; the region has experienced landslides and soil-covered roads, yards, and driveways; repeated Notices of Violation have been served; and the Virginia DEQ has shut down the MVP because the state's erosion and sediment control standards are not adequate to handle the siltation from a project of this magnitude.

The pipeline builders, EQT Corporation and Dominion, are not "doing it right."

I hear from the opposite side that these pipelines are safe. I'm not convinced.

A newly constructed thirty-two-inch pipeline exploded last month in West Virginia and incinerated eleven acres of land. In 2010 the San Bruno natural gas pipeline, near San Francisco, California, destroyed thirty-seven homes and killed eight people. In 2008 a natural gas pipeline explosion in Appomattox, Virginia, destroyed two homes.

Pipeline accidents resulted in 297 significant incidents in 2017 according to the U.S. Department of Transportation's Pipeline and Hazardous Materials Safety Administration, which defines "significant incident" as any fatality or damage exceeding fifty thousand dollars. In 2017 such incidents caused eight fatalities and damages exceeding two hundred million dollars.

Just because EQT and Dominion keep saying pipelines are safe does not make me believe it.

I've taken their other talking point, that having a pipeline under your property will not lower its value, with a grain of salt as well.

I see the news reports, I see the pictures of soil erosion, I hear the voices of the people affected and run over by profiteering corporations. The Virginia Department of Transportation closed Cahas Mountain Road in Franklin County because of mudslides that MVP construction caused.

MVP contractors were not supposed to cut trees after the beginning of the nesting season for migratory birds, yet they kept felling the trees, bird nests and all.

The ACP has conditional 401 certification from the Virginia State Water Control Board because it did not submit all the plans required by law, and yet it proceeded to cut down trees along the path of the pipeline. It did not follow the Federal Energy Regulatory Commission's instructions while cutting the trees. It was served a Notice of Violation because it cut trees too close to streams.

If Dominion can't follow directions for cutting down a tree, how can we trust the company to follow directions with the largest fracked gas pipeline in Virginia and the largest soil disturbance since the interstate highways were built?

The truth is we can't.

The sedimentation onto adjacent landscapes and into our streams during construction of these pipelines has been and will be a constant quagmire of pollution and injustice. If these projects move forward, they will cause unprecedented damage to our environment and a raft of lawsuits.

Below are my suggestions for how Governor Northam can "do it right" and avoid these very avoidable consequences.

First, he should halt all construction for the MVP and the ACP until FERC has completed a proper review as requested by Senator Tim Kaine and members of Congress from both parties. Many studies show that these pipelines are not needed.

Second, the administration should require the stream-by-stream, detailed construction plans for every stream and wetland crossing promised by our governor and demanded by the citizens of this Commonwealth. If Virginia's State Water Control Board cannot confirm that these plans will not violate state water quality standards, then it must deny 401 certification.

Dominion has a long history of disregard for the law. Dominion and EQT have received multiple Notices of Violation from Virginia and West Virginia.

Based on Dominion's track record for environmental stewardship, I don't believe for a moment that these pipelines can be built without violating our water quality standards and our rights.

Governor Northam, you and you alone can make this right. It's time for your administration and its agencies to put the citizens of this commonwealth—our health and safety—above the corporate interests putting us, and our environment, at risk.

Atlantic Coast Pipeline Set to Destroy Old-Growth Forest

This op-ed was published in the News Leader *on October 17, 2018.*

"At least three hundred trees, older than this nation will be destroyed if the Atlantic Coast Pipeline comes through this ridge on our property," Bill Limpert lamented. We were walking his part of Jack Mountain in Bath County, Virginia. I could smell the old-growth forest as we walked under the towering Sugar Maples, Shagbark Hickories, and Chestnut Oaks. The branches create a cathedral canopy seventy feet over our heads.

Bill and his wife, Lynn, named this part of Jack Mountain Miracle Ridge because it gives them a spiritual feeling, walking among the giant trees. I could not believe how steep the land was in every direction. The top of this ridge, or spur, leading up Jack Mountain, is a forty-six percent slope. The side slopes are steeper.

The one to the north is a seventy-eight percent slope. A human cannot walk on land this steep. If I dared to step off to the north, I would almost free-fall to the canyon floor one hundred feet below. The planned Atlantic Coast Pipeline (ACP) will unearth a swath of mayhem three thousand feet long and at least 125 feet wide through the Limpert's property.

"When this ridge leaves our property, it gets even steeper," Bill said. "The timber up there has never, ever, been cut."

The ACP, Dominion Energy's forty-two-inch-diameter, fracked-gas pipeline, is planned to come up this ridge and cross Jack Mountain. Dominion will have to cut down thousands of old-growth trees, clear a swath 125 feet wide, and dig a trench ten feet deep in the steepest terrain I have ever walked on in Virginia. This clearing will cause the most irresponsible environmental damage to this forest—ever. Loggers never touched it because it is so steep.

All the streams born on this land drain to Little Valley Run, a wild, native trout stream. If the pipeline is constructed, the sediment leaving the site will destroy the aquatic habitat necessary for Brook Trout to survive. The waters of Little Valley Run empty into Bolar Run, another native trout stream, then into the Jackson River, followed by the James River and into the Chesapeake Bay.

We stopped at one of the largest sugar maples in the path of the pipeline. Lynn Limpert named it Ona. It's between 260 and 300 years old. Here, we talked about all the folks that have come to see this forest, feel its energy, and ponder the plunder.

Bill retired from the Maryland Department of Environment in 2010. He was an area supervisor for erosion and sediment controls on construction jobs. He knows what he is talking about when he says the erosion and sediment control plans for this pipeline are woefully inadequate. "Dominion and DEQ should not attempt this," he says.

Virginia's Department of Environmental Quality (DEQ) holds the pipeline builders to the lowest possible erosion and sediment control standard—a two-year storm frequency. The Chesapeake

Bay Foundation, Appalachian Voices, Jackson River Preservation Association Inc., and many other environmental organizations sued the Virginia DEQ and the State Water Control Board for being arbitrary and capricious when they issued the 401 certification for the Atlantic Coast Pipeline. In short, the erosion and sediment controls for this massive pipeline are inadequate to protect Virginia's streams from sediment pollution.

The worst part of this saga may not be the insane notion of destroying the mountain by constructing the ACP but how Dominion has treated the Limperts, and many others in their way—with disrespect, unanswered questions, a subpoena to appear in court, and silence.

> TWO-YEAR STORM FREQUENCY *The amount of rainfall during a two-year, twenty-four-hour period for this part of Virginia is 3.5 inches. These data can be found in the National Weather Services Technical Paper 40:* Rainfall Frequency Atlas of the United States.

Survey crews damaged the Limpert's property, Dominion forced them into court, and generated reports that are "inaccurate, evasive, and misleading," according to the retired soil erosion inspector.

The Limperts have not accepted any offers from Dominion to compensate them for taking their land. There is no way to set a value on this needless, unwanted, and reckless destruction. They fear that they will receive a condemnation letter any day allowing Dominion to take their land by eminent domain.

"It's been an ongoing nightmare," Bill tells me.

What has our country come to?

A corporation can take your land by eminent domain—for profit. The pipeline builders can injure, maim, and kill federally endangered species. Construction of these pipelines has caused landslides, explosions, and sediment-filled streams and roads, violating Virginia's water quality standards. They ask the courts for "quick-take condemnation" of private land. I have seen them bring in outsiders to speak at hearings. They use "placeholders" in lines at hearings to prevent local people from speaking. Dominion paid in advance for "any and all future damages." Dominion Energy has a long history of disregarding the law.

Take, take, take is their credo.

We must stop the systemic and epidemic corporate creed taking place throughout this country. We must vote for candidates that will fight for people's rights and we must support the environmental groups fighting on the land and in the courts. So many people, like the Limperts, are being bullied and taken advantage of by corporations like Dominion Energy. Finally, we must continue to resist, peacefully demonstrate, and stand our ground as the Limperts are doing—true heroes for property rights and water quality.

Carbon Farming Mitigates Climate Change

While we often hear of new technology to address climate change, it is important to remember that farmers have been keeping carbon out of the atmosphere for countless generations. In what is sometimes called carbon farming, carbon dioxide is captured by plants and stored in the soil.

"How does this happen?" you ask.

Trees turn carbon into wood. Wheat turns carbon into straw. Grass turns carbon into protein for livestock. When farmers apply manure on the land as fertilizer, or when they turn a cover crop into the soil, or when they leave any plant residue on the land, they are putting carbon back into the soil.

In fact, U.S. farmland is capable of sequestering 650 million metric tons of carbon dioxide each year, offsetting eleven percent of America's greenhouse gas, according to a report published by the Soil Science Society of America. With so much potential, it is time to greatly expand carbon capture and offset programs.

The element carbon is found in virtually all forms of life on Earth. It is in all proteins, carbohydrates, fats, and all life's building blocks. Because of this, scientists call life on Earth carbon-based life forms. Carbon is the same element that binds with two atoms of oxygen to form carbon dioxide (CO_2)—what plants "breathe" in and humans breathe out.

Carbon dioxide is a byproduct of how we live. When we use fossil fuels for electricity or when we drive our cars, carbon dioxide and other pollutants wind up in the air. Carbon dioxide absorbs heat that the Earth reflects. As we humans emit more and more CO_2 into the atmosphere, the CO_2 absorbs more and more heat.

In September 2016, carbon dioxide levels in Earth's atmosphere reached their highest levels in four million years, exceeding four hundred parts per million. Reducing this concentration is the goal for a healthy planet for humans. Every nation on the planet except Syria and Nicaragua committed to this goal in 2015 by signing the Paris Climate Accord. Unfortunately, the United States intends to withdraw from the accord, although it cannot legally do so until November 4, 2020.

Syria and Nicaragua have since announced plans to join the accord leaving the United States as the only holdout on the entire planet.

But even if the U.S. government withdraws, we as individual citizens can do our part in helping the planet.

There are many ways to reduce carbon in the atmosphere.

First, we need to reduce the amount of carbon going into the atmosphere by switching to renewable electric energy and driving more fuel-efficient or electric cars. Reducing methane emissions from natural gas and rice production would also result in less carbon in the atmosphere.

Second, we need to capture the carbon that's in the atmosphere and put it back into the earth. Green plants and farmers have been doing this for centuries.

Plants are the lungs of our planet. They capture carbon in the atmosphere through photosynthesis. They breathe in CO_2, turn it into a sugar, and exhale oxygen. All green plants capture carbon and store it.

Carbon caps, credits, and trading programs are already in place in several states and in many foreign countries. For example, France's "four per thousand" program intends to pay farmers for increasing soil carbon.

Carbon farming is the act of leaving crop residues on the land or applying manure to the land. This increases soil organic matter, which in turn increases water infiltration to the soil, enhances nutrient cycling, reduces soil compaction and soil erosion, increases crop yields, feeds the soil ecosystem, and reduces CO_2 in the atmosphere.

Expanding efforts like creating carbon markets in the U.S. Farm Bill and other programs to increase carbon in the soil will help turn the tide against the damage from global warming and resulting climate change.

The Carbon in My Burning Log

The flames of the fire hold my senses hostage. Staring at the orange flames dancing upward, I hear the crackling release of carbon entombed in the hardened cell walls of the log. I feel the heat, a byproduct of the transfer of energy as the log is transformed from a solid to a gas. I stare. My mind wanders. . . . What happened the year the carbon was captured from the atmosphere to make this log perhaps a hundred years ago?

1918: Woodrow Wilson is president of the United States, the trenches of the Argonne are empty, and World War I ends. Fritz

Haber, a German physicist, is awarded the Nobel Prize for inventing the process to make nitrogen fertilizer from the air (the atmosphere is about seventy-eight percent nitrogen), the last captive Carolina Parakeet dies in the Cincinnati Zoo, Nelson Mandela is born, the carbon dioxide level in the atmosphere is 290 parts per million.

The carbon being released as a gas from the log I watch was a combination of cellulose, lignin, and hemicellulose, all complex compounds containing carbon.

The carbon cycle is one of the most important and profound ecosystem services on Earth. Plants take in carbon dioxide through photosynthesis and make sugars out of it. Animals eat the plants to make cells and grow. Animals die and their carbon-filled bodies are consumed by microbes in the soil.

Bury all the carbon-filled animals for a million years, add pressure, and presto, we have coal and crude oil—fossil fuels. One of the greatest functions of the soil beneath our feet is to capture, recycle, and store carbon. The soil is the largest terrestrial reservoir of carbon.

We often hear of the nutrients necessary for plant growth—nitrogen (N), phosphorous (P), and potassium (K)—but we don't hear much about carbon as a nutrient. We don't fertilize with carbon because plants take in carbon without human intervention.

In the past one hundred years, we humans have extracted trillions of tons of solid and liquid-entombed carbon from the depths of the Earth in the form of coal and crude oil. The world extracts and uses about nine billion tons of coal per year and about thirty-five billion barrels of crude oil per year. Humans have been on a fossil fuel binge economy since about 1900.

One of the byproducts of all this conversion is the release of carbon dioxide into the atmosphere. Carbon dioxide is one of the greenhouse gases that traps heat when it is reflected by the Earth's surface.

The last place on Earth without a four-hundred parts per million (ppm) CO_2 concentration was Antarctica, and in 2016 it crossed that threshold as well. The Earth has not had this much CO_2 in the atmosphere in four million years.

Fossil fuels have served humanity well, but it is time to move on. Scientists warn us that we need an atmosphere with a concentration of CO_2 no higher than 350 ppm. Higher concentrations of CO_2 cause our climate to change; warmer temperatures bring more violent storms, more wildfires, more droughts, and sea level rise.

Our challenge is to lower the concentration of CO_2 in the atmosphere. We can do this. First, by reducing carbon going into the air, and second, by capturing carbon in the air and putting it back into the earth. This is called carbon sequestration. The cool thing (pun intended) is that we can use plants to do this.

We need to put a cap on carbon emmisions. Many countries and now many U.S. states are establishing carbon diets for carbon-emitting practices such as coal-fired power plants, car and truck exhausts, and agricultural tillage. Once we establish the diets, we can then put a tax on carbon emissions that exceed these limits.

We can use revenue from the taxes or established carbon markets to create incentives for practices that sequester carbon, such as solar and wind energy, lower transportation emissions, reduced agricultural tillage, and carbon farming. This is called cap and trade.

One of the recently created carbon markets is the Regional Greenhouse Gas Initiative (RGGI)—the first mandatory market-based program in America to reduce greenhouse gas emissions. Nine New England and Atlantic states are members, including three Chesapeake Bay watershed states: Delaware, New York, and Maryland.

Legislation was introduced in 2018 in Virginia to arrange for the state to join the initiative, but the bill was killed in committee by representatives voting along party lines.

All Chesapeake Bay states should join the RGGI or create their own carbon markets because it will help restore the Bay and improve human health. Breathing cleaner air is good for us!

Save the Farm, Save the Bay

This op-ed piece was published by the Bay Journal News Service on April 19, 2016, and received an Excellence-in-Craft Award from the Virginia Outdoor Writers Association.

Where can you find the most cost-effective path to cleaner water in the Bay? Down on the farm, of course.

The five-year court battle is over. The Supreme Court of the United States, by declining to hear the case, has affirmed two lower court decisions stating that the U.S. Environmental Protection Agency did not overstep its bounds by setting total maximum daily loads (TMDL), or a "pollution diet," for jurisdictions in the Chesapeake Bay watershed

That is now settled law, part of the federal Clean Water Act, and we can finally focus our resources on what will make the most difference to the health of the Bay: improving soil health on farmland and cleaning up our streams. It is now time for environmentalists, farmers, bureaucrats, politicians, and watermen in the Chesapeake Bay watershed to embrace this fact: A well-managed farm is the most important land use and our greatest hope for a restored Bay.

The first order of business is to keep farmers on the farm. The second order of business is to help farmers apply the necessary soil and water conservation measures on their land so that soil and nutrients stay on their land, out of their local streams, and out of the Bay. Not counting forested land, farmland has, by far, the largest footprint in the Bay's sixty-four-thousand-square-mile watershed and, happily, it is the most economical and practical land to treat for clean water. For sure, the Bay has many other sources of pollution, and many efforts are underway to eliminate them, but farmland has the most potential to do the most good.

The following scenario is true and is typical of what happens somewhere, every day, in this sprawling watershed. A two-hundred-acre farm in the Shenandoah Valley is rezoned from agriculture to high-density residential. Developers bulldoze the green pastures, put up four hundred houses and people move in . . . a thousand of them. The larger population requires a new elementary school and a sewage treatment plant upgrade that together cost the taxpayers in the county more than thirty million dollars. It also takes away another piece of what makes the Shenandoah Valley so beautiful—farmland.

I wish we would instead give the farmer a million dollars to not develop. This alternative would save twenty-nine million dollars in public funds.

Protecting farmland from development is the best way to avoid the cost of future development. The more farmland in the watershed, the easier it will be to put locally grown, healthy food on the table and restore the Bay. Farmland not only produces food, fiber, feed, and fuel, it can also produce clean water, if it is managed properly.

When it rains on farmland where good soil and water conservation measures are in place, the rain soaks into the soil, percolates through it, and emerges as clean water in our streams. The soil regulates the water cycle. Not so with concrete, pavement, and rooftops from urban areas. The resulting runoff from these areas is not clean water; it is the most expensive and difficult water to treat.

So our greatest hope, and the best value for our money, is to help farmers stay on the farm and continue their work to improve soil health on their land. Agriculture is halfway to reducing its share of nutrients fouling local streams and eventually reaching the Bay. That's why the Virginia General Assembly recently passed a budget with an estimated thirty million dollars for land conservation and 61.7 million dollars for agricultural best management practices. To varying degrees, other Bay states are investing in farmland preservation and improvements as well.

Land conservation involves a mixture of incentives and disincentives to encourage farmers to keep their farms in place and operational instead of selling the land for nonfarm uses. Outright purchase of development rights is one way to conserve farmland,

and various federal, state, and local tax incentives can help farms stay in agricultural production.

Beyond that, we need to greatly expand financial aid and incentives for agricultural best management practices that minimize farm runoff and pollution. These practices include rotational grazing, using cover crops to protect the soil during the winter, planting on the contour, rotating crops, keeping livestock out of streams, and carefully managing nutrients. The cost of government support of these practices pales in comparison to the expense of upgrading a wastewater treatment plant or reducing urban and suburban polluted runoff.

Where do farmers need help? Where they have overgrazed pastures, eroding cropland, manure-laden feedlots with streams flowing past or through them, livestock lounging in streams, and too many nutrients applied to fields; those are the main causes of agricultural pollution. But we have well-known fixes for these poor practices and funds to help get the job done.

The U.S. Supreme Court has ruled: The Chesapeake Clean Water Blueprint is our path forward. The blueprint is online. Every state, every county, and every city knows its part in restoring the Bay. Let's work together to show the world that we really can restore the Chesapeake Bay.

Madison, Montpelier, and a Constitutional Amendment for the Environment

I could hardly see daylight through the massive trunks of trees. Tulip Poplars, White Oaks, and Shagbark Hickories nourished from deep, rich soil towered over me as I walked in the Landmark Forest at Montpelier. This is old-growth forest. As I walk and smell the damp humus-filled woodland, I breathe in the history, culture, and ecology of this place.

Montpelier, home of James Madison, fourth president of the United States, author of our Constitution, and architect of the Bill of Rights, was the setting for a "Design Congress," organized by Nelson Byrd Woltz Landscape Architects and hosted by the staff of Montpelier in the Robert H. Smith Center for the Constitution.

What a fitting place for such an event. Our mission was to create a new vision for the 2,650-acre landscape. But much more was achieved. The seeds of a renewed environmental movement took root; seeds that were planted by Madison himself: The words from his 1818 speech to his farming neighbors became the foundation of our vision for a renewed Montpelier landscape.

Here's a teaser:

> *There is a known tendency in all organized beings to multiply beyond the degree necessary to keep up their actual numbers.*

His words are as relevant today as they were in his time and perhaps as important as the U.S. Constitution.

It was the speech Madison gave to his fellow farmers in the Agricultural Society of Albemarle when he became the organization's president on May 12, 1818. The speech contained a list of seven "instructions."

As I read them for the first time, I thought, If we had only put these words to work, we would not have impaired waters, toxic algae blooms, and giant dead zones in our estuaries and the Gulf of Mexico.

Madison was keenly aware that the "slash and burn" American model of farming exhausted the productivity of the soil, not only in Virginia but across the new nation. We cut most of our timber, annihilated species, and migrated west to find more productive soil. How could we better manage our soil at home and produce what was necessary to feed a hungry nation?

Madison's seven instructions are listed below. I have elaborated under each one.

1. The error first to be noticed is that of cultivating land, either naturally poor or improvised by cultivation.

The production of annual crops has inherent risks, especially for soil erosion. The more we cultivate the land, the more risk of erosion. Reducing tillage, using cover crops, and planting on the contour reduces this risk.

2. The evil of pressing too hard on the land, has also been much increased by the bad mode of ploughing it.

Soil productivity is like a bank account. If we continue to take from the account without putting back, eventually we will have nothing left. Continuously plowing and cultivating the soil exhausts its productivity.

3. The neglect of manures is another error which claims particular notice.

Plant residues and animal manures are valuable ingredients for healthy soil. They contain many nutrients including carbon. The soil plays a major role in the carbon cycle. In fact, the soil can hold more carbon than all the plants put together and can be a major carbon sink to help stem climate change.

4. Among the means of aiding the productiveness of the soil, which have not received merited attention, is irrigation.

Improving irrigation efficiencies and using more drought-tolerant crops are keys to sustainability.

5. I cannot but consider it as an error in our husbandry, that oxen are too little used in place of horses.

Madison teaches us to continually improve. Moving from the horse to the oxen is now like transitioning from the plow to no-till or moving from annuals to perennials.

6. A more manifest error in the husbandry of the older settlements is that of keeping too many neat cattle on the farms. As a farm should not be cultivated farther than it can be continued in good heart; the stock of cattle should not be in greater number than the resources of food will keep in good plight.

This is one of our greatest challenges: to not exceed the carrying capacity of the land. A classic example today is the "Big Chicken—No Land" movement sweeping the Eastern Shore. This is when a farmer puts five huge poultry houses on a small piece of land that cannot possibly use the manure generated from the operation. Another example is when we have more livestock on the land than the land can support, which leads to confined animal feeding operations that in turn lead to an imbalance of nutrients.

7. Of all the errors in our rural economy, none is perhaps so much to be regretted, because none so difficult to be repaired, as the injudicious and excessive destruction of timber and fire wood.

This is especially true along streams. Riparian forest buffers are one of the most cost-effective best management practices. To restore the health of our streams, we need to plant millions of native trees along their banks.

The people who work the land need Madison's instructions.

Fertilizer runoff from cropland has caused toxic algae blooms in Lake Erie, and the second largest dead zone in the world, mainly the result of agricultural runoff into the Mississippi River, is in the Gulf of Mexico. The American Farm Bureau and other deep-pocketed lobbyists with industries tied to pollution sued the

Environmental Protection Agency *(American Farm Bureau Federation v. EPA)* because the states in the Chesapeake Bay watershed have a plan to clean up the streams that feed the Bay. And to top that, the U.S. Farm Bill allows farmers to receive USDA benefits even if the land they work is eroding at twice the rate agronomists know is sustainable.

It's time to put Madison's words to work to restore our streams, rivers, estuaries, and our land.

The agricultural team of the Design Congress offered this vision statement:

To honor the legacy of James Madison as an environmentalist by demonstrating an ethics of democratic and transformative landscape through agriculture, ecology, and culture.

Many things will change in the landscape at Montpelier in the coming years. Beyond the mansion, visitor center, Landmark Forest, and many trails, visitors will be able to see, touch, smell, taste, and feel the agriculture that Madison practiced and envisioned. Visitors will be able to feel the culture of slavery, hard work, and science. And maybe, just maybe, a constitutional convention will be held here, in this special place, to create a constitutional amendment for humanity and the environment.

Lake Erie Heart Attack

This is an op-ed piece I wrote for the Bay Journal News Service that was distributed on August 19, 2014.

A heart attack is a huge wake-up call, that if you survive it, usually warrants a change of diet. Toledo, Ohio, just survived a heart attack! The city's drinking water from Lake Erie became toxic because of a huge algae bloom. Algae blooms are caused by too much nitrogen and phosphorous in the water. It's Toledo's wake-up call, and it's time for a change of lifestyle.

Small amounts of the algae that caused Toledo's heart attack are naturally present in most water bodies including all the Great Lakes, the Chesapeake Bay, Albemarle Sound, and the Gulf of Mexico. Too much nitrogen and or phosphorus (nutrients) can cause these algae to grow to enormous sizes. Called blooms, these masses of algae give off toxic substances that harm humans, wildlife, and the aquatic ecosystem. Algae blooms are also responsible for dead zones—areas in water bodies so depleted of oxygen that nothing can live.

Nitrogen and phosphorus are major components in fertilizer, manure, and sewage. Improper use and disposal of these nutrients contaminates our streams when rainwater washes off agricultural fields, feedlots, lawns, and golf courses. Failing septic systems and outdated wastewater treatment plants also contribute to excessive nutrients in streams.

Reducing nutrients in our streams and rivers is the cure; some call this a pollution diet. We have one of these diets underway right now in the Chesapeake Bay watershed, and it is working. Nitrogen and phosphorous levels in the Chesapeake Bay have been cut in half since the mid-1980s, despite the thirty percent increase in the Bay watershed's population—from thirteen and a half million in 1985 to seventeen million in 2012. This is an incredible achievement! The diet is working.

Reducing nutrients in streams is not rocket science. We know how to do it. Each of the six states in the Bay watershed came up with its own pollution diet to reduce nutrient loading into its streams and rivers. The Environmental Protection Agency approved these six plans several years ago, and together they form the Chesapeake Clean Water Blueprint.

Lots of people are working together to implement the blueprint. Farmers are fencing their cows out of the streams, planting riparian buffers, using fertilizers more responsibly, and reducing soil erosion by using no-till methods and cover crops during the winter.

Local and state governments are investing in sewage treatment upgrades that remove nutrients from their discharges. People in cities and suburban areas are using less fertilizer on their lawns. Legislatures are passing laws encouraging nutrient management and have eliminated phosphorous in lawn fertilizers. Citizens are paying stormwater utility fees to help fund stormwater management projects.

But deep-pocketed lobbyists from outside the Bay watershed don't like the pollution diet for the Bay. The Fertilizer Institute, the American Farm Bureau Federation, the Corn Growers Association, the National Pork Producers Council, the National Chicken Council, the National Association of Home Builders, and other lobbying groups associated with activities that contribute to nutrient loading are suing the Environmental Protection Agency over the plan to restore the Chesapeake Bay.

Even more disturbing, the attorneys general in twenty-one states, most of them in the Mississippi watershed, signed "friend of the court" briefs on behalf of these deep-pocketed lobbyists. Meanwhile, Toledo residents can't use their water, and the dead zone in the Gulf of Mexico remains the second largest in the world.

Clean water is a choice. The people of the Chesapeake Bay watershed have agreed on a plan for a cleaner Bay. Successful implementation will result in safer and more abundant seafood, more jobs, and increased tourism. We will have a healthier world; something of which we can be proud.

I lament that we have to waste time and money on a lawsuit because we want and need cleaner water.

What happened in Toledo is unfortunate and tragic. For a remedy, they need look no further than the Chesapeake Clean Water Blueprint. It's a pollution diet that is working.

Well-Managed 'Open Space' Should Not Be Taxed

This is an op-ed piece that was distributed by the Bay Journal News Service on June 6, 2015.

Well-managed farmland and other working "open spaces" should not be taxed when they provide ecosystem services exceeding the cost of public services for the land.

In many states, including Virginia, local governments have a special way of collecting revenue from their constituents who have a farm or open-space designation. Called land-use taxation, it's a method of calculating a tax based on the way the land is used and the quality of the soil. It benefits farmers because it taxes them only modestly for their pasture, cropland, and forest.

These landowners are still taxed like everyone else for their residences, barns, outbuildings, tenant houses, and other structures. The open space I refer to is only the land that is used for pasture, cropland, forest, or other working landscapes that provide ecosystem services.

Now, for the record, some open spaces may receive land-use tax rates that, in my opinion, shouldn't—lands that have been retired from food and fiber production and have morphed into large manicured lawns with big houses. Large-lot residences are most often the costliest of all land uses because they fail to pay the true cost of the public services they demand, such as public sewer and water hook-ups. Countless "cost of community services" studies prove this.

Many think that land-use taxation is a tax break for farmers. I disagree. For working landscapes with pasture, cropland, forests, and wildlife habitat, I would like to offer an alternative to land-use taxation: not taxing these working lands at all. In fact, the landowners should be receiving credit for all the ecosystem services that their lands provide to the rest of us.

Allow me to make my case.

First, let me define "well managed." I am talking about open spaces that perform several functions. First, these landscapes build healthy soil; it's not eroding and washing into streams. Second, nutrient management is rigidly applied on these lands; nutrients do not run off into streams or seep into the groundwater. Third, the land has functioning riparian buffers along streams and hosts wildlife habitats. In other words, the land meets what the USDA calls a Total Resource Management Plan.

Granted, some lands don't come close to being well managed. But a lot of them do, so hear me out.

Well-managed farms provide far more ecosystem services to the public than they receive in public services. The soil regulates the entire hydrologic cycle. It's the carbon filter for our groundwater. Without this groundwater recharge area, we would have no groundwater; it would mostly just run off the land and into streams and rivers. How much is that recharging worth? Our current economy does not factor in most ecosystem services.

Healthy soil can also store a lot of carbon by leaving crop residues on the land and by manure application. Many sources say the soil can hold twice what plants can.

Farmland provides wildlife habitat and pollinator corridors.

Farms with riparian forest buffers supply clean water downstream. Streams with native trees along their banks are much more capable of detoxifying themselves than streams with no trees.

Here in the Shenandoah Valley, farmland provides amazing viewsheds that help drive the tourist industry. What are all these ecosystem services worth? I suggest that it is more than that land receives from the locality in the form of services. Do the cows get on the school bus? Does the land require garbage pickup or police protection? Does the land require public roads? Does the land require public water and sewer? On the contrary, that land is providing us with water. The fence along

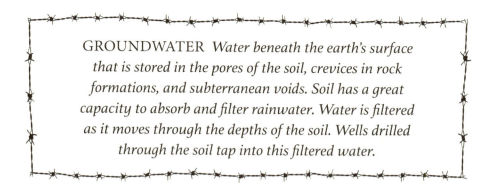

GROUNDWATER *Water beneath the earth's surface that is stored in the pores of the soil, crevices in rock formations, and subterranean voids. Soil has a great capacity to absorb and filter rainwater. Water is filtered as it moves through the depths of the soil. Wells drilled through the soil tap into this filtered water.*

the stream and that watering trough for the cows are far cheaper than the sewage treatment plant that would have to be built if the farmer sold all that land for a housing development.

Think of the development costs to taxpayers if the farmland were converted to a housing development. The taxpayers would have to pay for a new school, an upgrade for the sewage treatment plant, pipeline for water and sewer, landfill space, and on and on.

Here's a proposal, and let's allow landowners to decide which path to take. If farmers and landowners have well-managed farmland, let society pay them for the ecosystem services they provide. If farmers and landowners don't manage their farms well, let's help them do so. And for those few farmers and landowners who don't want a well-managed farm, let them pay a higher tax—after all, we pay to clean up the polluted water leaving their land.

Hugh Hammond Bennett, the father of soil conservation in America, said, "Society as a whole benefits from good land use; therefore, society as a whole should help pay for it."

Well-managed land provides ecosystem services including water filtration, carbon sequestration, wildlife habitat, and stream detoxification. If the land is performing these vital environmental tasks, why should the landowner be taxed for them?

When all our land is "well managed," we will no longer have dead zones in the Chesapeake Bay or the Gulf of Mexico. Our streams will be healthier, the Chesapeake Bay will be restored, and we will have a thriving economy.

Harpers Ferry—A History Steeped in Irony

I'm standing in the middle of the footbridge across the Potomac River at Harpers Ferry looking downstream. Beneath me flows the nation's river that at this point in its journey has drained six million acres of land.

Just downstream, and to my right, are the waters draining another two million acres. They join the Potomac. It's the Shenandoah River. Our farm, 135 miles upstream, is part of the beginning of that river.

The Potomac will empty into the Chesapeake Bay 165 miles downstream from this bridge.

Harpers Ferry is a magical place. In 1783 Jefferson wrote, "The passage of the Patowmac through the Blue Ridge is perhaps one of the most stupendous scenes in nature." Indeed, seeing all this water vent through the "hole" in the Blue Ridge Mountains is magnificent.

All this water generated power for one the country's first industrial complexes and one of our nation's largest armories before the American Civil War.

It was here in 1803 that Captain Meriwether Lewis purchased rifles, ammunition, and other supplies for the Lewis and Clark expedition, and it was here that in 1859 abolitionist John Brown lit one of the fuses that ignited the American Civil War, the conflagration that led to the end of slavery.

The history of Harpers Ferry is steeped in irony. Today the water in the river is clear and so is our path for the equality of human rights for all. It wasn't so clear in October of 1859 when John Brown and his band of men captured the U.S. Arsenal here and took hostages in hopes of inciting a slave insurrection.

Brown's plan failed. Colonel Robert E. Lee of the U.S. Marines captured the raiders the next day. Lee would later become general of the Army of Northern Virginia for the Confederacy.

John Brown was convicted of treason. He was hanged in Charles Town, Virginia (shortly to become West Virginia). John Wilkes Booth, who later assassinated Abraham Lincoln, witnessed the hanging.

I've been on this bridge when the waters were as brown as a chocolate milkshake. Sediment, nutrients, pathogens, and toxins enter the water upstream because of poor land use. Polluted water hurts everyone downstream. We know what pollutes the water and the Chesapeake Bay, and we know how to clean it up, yet so many people just don't care or are not willing to manage their land so they don't harm those downstream. After all, what we do on our land directly affects the water leaving our land.

But we have good news too. Streams throughout the Bay watershed are being removed from the nation's dirty waters lists because the people in those streamsheds are banding together to clean them up. One of the best efforts to help the Bay is farmers fencing their livestock out of their streams and installing riparian buffers. Wastewater treatment plants are being upgraded throughout the watershed, and when streams get clean enough, native trout are coming back.

The path to restored streams and the Chesapeake Bay is clear. We need to keep this effort going, and we need to persuade more people to do their part. The Chesapeake Bay is on its way to being restored. How about the stream in your backyard or on your farm?

Tree Swallows, Mercury Contamination, and the Middle River

There are many harbingers of spring in Swoope; the yellow blooms of Daffodils and Forsythia, the sounds of Spring Peepers, and pastures changing from brown to green are only a few. My favorite harbinger of spring is the arrival of Tree Swallows. I start looking for them in late February. This year they arrived in Swoope on March 18.

Our Tree Swallows migrated almost two thousand miles north from Florida and Cuba. They come here to breed and raise their young, returning south in the fall.

We maintain forty-eight nest boxes for them and other cavity nesters such as Eastern Bluebirds and Carolina Chickadees. There must be a hundred Tree Swallows along Trimbles Mill Road and the Middle River. We often see two or three birds around each nest box.

Anytime we drive a truck or tractor into a pasture, it disturbs insects. The Tree Swallows come to get them. Barn Swallows, Cliff Swallows, and Northern Rough-Winged Swallows join the feeding frenzy. It's an amazing show of flight with colorful dives and swoops.

We have always had a few nest boxes, but in 2005 Dan Cristol, chancellor professor of biology from the College of William & Mary, asked us to participate in a research project to study the biomagnification of mercury up the food chain. He and his students put up hundreds of nest boxes along the Middle, South, and North Rivers in Augusta County. On our farm, they added thirty nest boxes to the ones we already had.

Waynesboro, Virginia, was the site of a DuPont synthetic fiber production plant that discharged mercury into the South River from 1930 to 1950. The South River is the southernmost branch of the Shenandoah River. The Middle and North Rivers were used as reference sites in Cristol's research because they didn't have legacy mercury discharges in the river.

Tree Swallows were Cristol's main species of study because during the breeding season they eat only flying insects. Insects such as Mayflies, Dragonflies, Caddisflies, and Stoneflies spend their immature life in streams and rivers. The ones in the South River spent their aquatic life in the sediments contaminated with mercury. When these aquatic insects hatch from the water and become flying insects, many are eaten by Tree Swallows. The swallows then feed these insects to their babies, which, in turn, ingest the mercury

Cristol's groundbreaking research was published in the April 2008 edition of *Science* magazine. The article, "The Movement of Aquatic Mercury Through Terrestrial Food Webs," states that "mercury is a persistent contaminant that biomagnifies up the food web, causing mortality, reproductive failure, and other health effects in predatory wildlife and humans."

Cristol's studies proved that mercury, in fact, does biomagnify up the food chain and revealed that mercury is twenty times higher than in the reference birds on our river.

One research paper attests that the six years of field research that Cristol's groups did was probably "the first study to suggest disruption of multiple endocrine functions by mercury in wild animals." Cristol and his students published over fifty papers on their findings of mercury in wildlife.

"The mercury-exposed swallows suffer a reduced hormonal response to stress, altered thyroid hormone levels, suppressed immune system, twenty percent fewer offspring annually, and, most interestingly, a greatly reduced ability to withstand heat waves. Normally hot weather is great for them because of the increased number of insects flying around, but on the contaminated sites, that is when the babies tended to die ... so there is trouble ahead when mercury and global climate change run into each other," Cristol wrote.

The William & Mary field research ended in 2010, but we still maintain the nest boxes and added even more. It is a joy to see the birds, with their metallic blue-green upper bodies and white breasts, flying around the pastures pursuing insects.

The William & Mary research was used as part of the South River–South Fork Shenandoah River Natural Resources Damage Assessment Plan that led to a settlement from DuPont of forty-eight million dollars distributed to various environmental organizations to improve our landscape and waters. This is the largest natural resource damage settlement in Virginia history and the eighth largest in U.S. history.

The College of William & Mary was a member of the South River Science Team that used research to understand, educate, and reduce the effects of mercury in the South River. We are very proud to have been a small part of this massive research project that resulted in some form of environmental justice for the decades of mercury contamination of a major river.

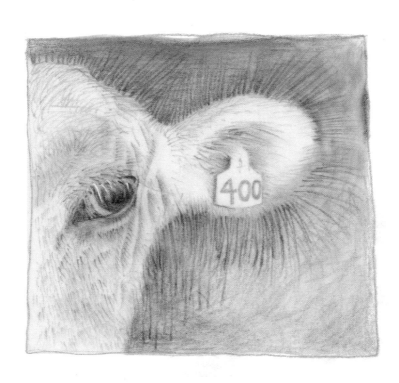

9
Hope for Agriculture

2XT: Farm Bill Bad News for Soil Sustainability

The Story of 2XT and Allan Bocock

Allan Bocock was a grain farmer in Stuarts Draft, Virginia. Each year, he planted over one thousand acres of annual crops, including corn, soybeans, wheat, and barley. I met Allan in the late eighties when I moved to the Shenandoah Valley of Virginia as a District Conservationist for the Soil Conservation Service (SCS). This is the true story of how he built healthy soil from excessively eroded land and how the next farmer destroyed it all.

We first met during the rollout of the 1985 Farm Bill known as the Food Security Act. It was the first time in U.S. history that USDA benefits to farmers were tied to soil conservation. As a result of this law, soil conservationists in the Soil Conservation Service were responsible for identifying land where annual crops grew on what was labeled "Highly Erodible Land." Once we identified the land, we informed landowners of our determination and then calculated their current rate of soil erosion. I was in charge of this process in the local soil and water conservation district.

How much soil can one afford to lose through the acts of erosion and still maintain productivity indefinitely? The term for this in soil science is the "tolerance value" or "T" for short.

It's expressed as tons per acre per year. A ton of soil covering one acre—roughly the size of a football field—is about the thickness of a sheet of paper. T values range from one to five tons per acre per year. All the soils in the United States have been mapped, named, and analyzed. T values has been assigned for every soil. The data is online at www.websoilsurvey.sc.egov.usda.gov.

The first step in soil conservation on annual cropland is to make sure soil erosion is at a soil's T value or less. For example, if a soil's T value is two, that field can afford to lose up to two tons of soil per acre per year and still maintain productivity because natural processes will make two tons of soil per acre per year. If one farms in a manner that reduces erosion below the T value, then the land experiences a net gain in soil. This is the sweet spot in soil conservation—building soil. In contrast, farming in a manner that exceeds the T value creates soil movement downslope. Inevitably this soil will enter a ditch or nearby stream and become sediment, the largest pollutant by volume in America's streams, rivers, estuaries, and lakes.

Congressional debate before the passage of the 1985 Food Security Act was exhaustive. Environmentalists argued that soil erosion on annual cropland should be at the tolerance level for Highly Erodible Land to receive USDA benefits.

Many farmers and their lobbyists, on the other hand, didn't want to have anything to do with more regulation. Farmers loathe the thought of some government bureaucrat calculating the amount of soil erosion taking place on their crop fields.

In soil conservation, we calculate a farmer's average annual soil loss by using the Universal Soil Loss Equation (USLE). Six factors guide us in developing a cropping system that reduces soil loss to sustainable levels, or to T. When I started with the Soil Conservation Service in 1980, we used a slide rule to make the calculations. Today, we use a computer, and as one can imagine, it has become much more complicated.

The result was what I call the great soil erosion compromise: The U.S. Farm Bill, to this day, allows farmers to have twice the soil erosion on their Highly Erodible Land than what soil scientists believe is sustainable. We refer to this as two times T or 2XT.

Although arguably a good example of compromise and democracy, the result remains a deplorable example of sustainability.

During the rollout of the Farm Bill, I determined that Allan Bocock was indeed planting annual crops on Highly Erodible Land. Following government procedure at the time, I sent him a certified letter informing him of this determination. Even worse, he was farming a shallow soil, born from shale and highly erodible. This soil has a T value of two tons per acre per year.

It was a warm and sunny day when I met Allan. I drove along a dirt road to his farm and turned into the driveway to his shop. He was a tall, slender man in his late thirties with dark hair and a mustache. Hard at work, he had black engine grease on his hands. He wiped his hands with a rag and extended one to me.

He seemed eager to show me around the farm. We got into his small pickup truck and drove around to each crop field. I used the USLE slide rule calculator to predict the current average annual soil loss on each field as we went.

Allan was farming each crop field in one crop. Wheat here, corn there, soybeans somewhere else, and he was using tillage only when he thought it was necessary. His average annual soil losses were high—exceeding 9XT or over eighteen tons of soil loss per acre per year. He was on a downward slope to ruin. As the land loses more and more soil, the soil's productivity decreases, and farmers need more inputs like fertilizer to produce the same yields as the year before. The top ton of soil is the most productive ton, and his top ton was leaving the farm.

We would have to enlist every best management practice I knew to get him down to T. When I explained to Allan about soil health and his calculated soil losses, he understood. He wanted to build soil, not have it wash away into nearby streams.

He was an excellent candidate for contour-strip cropping. Contour farming (across the slope of the land) alone reduces erosion by half and increases soil moisture at least twofold. If these strips, or bands, of crops are alternated with bands of perennial crops, that reduces soil erosion by half again. By adding no-till cover crops, and leaving crop residues on the land, we could start the process of building soil and soil health. It took us several years to lay out all his cropland in contour strips.

What resulted was a beautiful landscape—sinuous bands of annual and perennial crops winding their way across the Shenandoah Valley slopes. It was a conservation cropping system; a combination of conservation measures in concert, working to produce food, healthy soil, and clean water.

Allan was not only in compliance with the Farm Bill, he was on his way to lowering his input costs and earning higher profits. As soil productivity increases, so does profit. As time went on, Allan came to see me several times and told me his yields were going up and his soils were improving.

A couple of decades later Allan and his wife bought a farm in the Midwest and moved. He rented all his Virginia farms to another farmer under the condition that the farmer remain in compliance with the Farm Bill.

That farmer came to see me. He said he wanted to take the contour strips out and plant all the fields in just one annual crop, and he would use pure no-till in all his operations.

I told him I didn't think that would work on those very erosive soils but would run the numbers and get back to him.

Well, since the first time I worked with Allan in the late eighties, the Universal Soil Loss Equation had undergone two revisions. We were in the process of being certified in using the new "Revised Universal Soil Loss Equation II," or RUSLE II for short.

Using the new figures in RUSLE II, the new farmer had an average annual soil loss of four tons per acre per year. In other words, he met the provisions of the 1985 Food Security Act—2XT.

How could this be? He was using only one conservation measure on the most erosive soil in the county, yet he was in compliance with America's Farm Bill. RUSLE II, I found out, gives little to no credit for contour or contour strip cropping when no-till is used.

I tried my best to convince that farmer that what he was about to do was not sustainable. We talked about building soil and productivity. We talked about runoff and soil erosion.

My salesmanship skills were insufficient, and much to my chagrin, that farmer ripped out all the contours, all the strip cropping, and all the perennial crops and replaced them with one annual crop. Reduced tillage and no-till are good practices, but we should not rely on these alone to do the important job of building healthy soil and improving water quality.

That farmer and many others like him are able to continue receiving USDA benefits while their calculated annual soil loss is twice what we know is sustainable.

The U.S. Farm Bill is renewed every five years. It's time to change the requirements in the law so that farmers receiving USDA benefits must meet soil erosion levels on annual crop fields that are at T or below.

 The Queen Bean, Tofu, and Dead Zones

This op-ed piece was distributed by the Bay Journal News Service on April 21, 2015.

Tofu. That's what most people think soybeans are grown for. But most soybeans in the United States are grown for oil and livestock feed.

It's big business. The United States is the world's largest producer and exporter of soybeans, with almost seventy-five million acres planted annually. Beans are second only to corn, planted on roughly eighty-four million acres.

The top ten soybean producing states are all in the Mississippi River watershed. Illinois grows more soybeans than any other U.S. state. In 2014, farmers in the Prairie State produced more than half a million bushels of beans.

Farm lobbying groups and farmers in the Midwest are gravely concerned that the EPA will force them to implement conservation practices like those required of farmers in the Chesapeake Bay watershed, practices like soil conservation and nutrient management that keep soil, nutrients, and pesticides on the land instead of allowing them to run off into nearby ditches, streams, and rivers.

Soybeans. Way more complicated than you think. This famous legume from China can produce more oil and protein per acre than almost any other plant on the planet. Lots of products are made from soybeans: oils, margarine, biodiesel fuel, candles, adhesives—even shoes are made from soybeans, and yes, tofu. You've heard of "King Corn"; well now there's "Queen Bean."

Most of the soybeans in the nation are "Roundup ready." These seeds have been genetically engineered to tolerate being sprayed with the herbicide Roundup. The grower plants Roundup-ready soybeans, waits for the weeds and his beans to emerge, sprays the whole field with Roundup, and the weed problem disappears.

Soybeans are a phenomenally versatile plant and much in demand. As with all annually planted crops, soil conservation and nutrient management are a must to keep what farmers pay dearly for, fertilizer and pesticides, from leaching into groundwater or running off the land into nearby ditches, streams, and rivers. Soybean fields are especially vulnerable to both leaching and runoff. The steeper the land, the more conservation measures are needed to prevent polluted runoff.

Combinations of practices such as no-till farming, planting on the contour, cover crops, crop rotation, contour strip farming, and nutrient management are very effective at preventing soil erosion and reducing water runoff. The simple practice of planting on the contour can reduce the likelihood of soil erosion by half.

In the Chesapeake Bay watershed, farmers are expected to implement not only soil conservation practices but also nutrient management practices to help us restore the streams where we live and where the water ends up, in the nation's largest estuary. Some sources say our farmers are already halfway to achieving their share of nutrient and sediment reduction strategies. Thank you, Chesapeake Bay watershed farmers!

But not everyone is on board with doing their part to clean up our nation's rivers. In *American Farm Bureau v. U.S. Environmental Protection Agency*, the American Farm Bureau, the Fertilizer Institute, the National Corn Growers Association, the National Chicken Council, and other deep-pocketed lobbying groups are suing the Environmental Protection Agency over the plans each state in the Chesapeake Bay watershed submitted to restore the Bay. These lobbyists lost in Federal District Court and have appealed to the U.S. Third Circuit Court of Appeals.

Recently, the Illinois Soybean Association sent a group of its growers to the Eastern Shore of Maryland and Delaware to investigate how the Chesapeake Clean Water Blueprint was working and how similar environmental actions would affect soybean growers in Illinois and other states in the Mississippi River watershed. According to an article in *Farm Futures*, Chesapeake Bay regulations would "flood" the Midwest, and the growers were "spooked" by all the regulations and requirements needed to clean up the Chesapeake Bay.

I have witnessed a lot of soil erosion from soybeans being planted on sloping fields. Soybeans are usually harvested late in the fall, which is often too late to plant winter cover crops. Soybean

---

AMERICAN FARM BUREAU V. U.S. EPA *The American Farm Bureau, et al., sued the EPA over the Chesapeake Clean Water Blueprint or TMDL for three reasons: using flawed science, overstepping its bounds, and not having a long enough comment period. On July 6, 2015, the plaintiffs lost again, and on February 29, 2016, the U.S. Supreme Court refused to see the case, leaving the blueprint intact and the law of the land in the Third Circuit Court.*

residue (what's left after the beans are harvested) has a low carbon-to-nitrogen ratio so it breaks down, or decomposes, much faster than corn stalks. This leaves a high percentage of the field bare. Bare soil through the winter is a recipe for disastrous soil erosion and runoff.

I can understand why soybean growers in the Midwest would be concerned. They might have to implement conservation practices to keep their soil, nutrients, and pesticides where they belong—on the land and not in the streams that feed the Mississippi River. The nutrients and soil transported by the Mississippi River from eroding farm fields into the Gulf of Mexico are, together, the number one cause for the second largest dead zone in the world.

Contour Farming: One of the Simplest and Most Effective Best Management Practices

In our quest to profit from the land and feed a hungry planet with annual crops such as corn and soybeans, we have abandoned one of the most powerful conservation practices known to science—contour farming. Used since ancient times to slow the flow of water across the land so it soaks into the soil, contour farming is a method of planting crops across the slope of the land or perpendicular to the flow of water.

The simple act of planting across the slope instead of up and down the hill does two very important things: it captures at least twice the rainwater and reduces soil erosion up to eightfold.

With the coming of "no-till" farming, I witnessed farmers taking out their contoured, curving bands of crops and abandoning the practice of planting on the contour. It is easier to just plant in the most expeditious manner, whether up and down the hill or around and around the field. Unfortunately, this faster method captures less water, which is a priceless asset for crops in July and August.

The 1938 *Yearbook of Agriculture, Soils and Men* includes a table showing the results of an experiment monitoring the effect of eleven inches of rainfall on farm fields. The field that was planted on the contour captured 6.7 inches of the rain; the noncontoured field captured only 2.1 inches.

Thomas Jefferson and Contour Farming: In a letter to William A. Burwell in 1810, Jefferson wrote, "We have had the most devastating rain which has ever fallen within my knowledge. Three inches of water fell in the space of about an hour. Every hollow of every hill presented a torrent which swept everything before it. I have never seen the fields so much injured. Mr. Randolph's farm is the only one which has not suffered; his horizontal furrows arrested the water at every step till it was absorbed. . . . Everybody in this neighborhood is adopting his method of ploughing, except tenants who have no interest in the preservation of the soil."

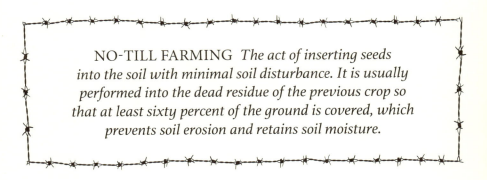

NO-TILL FARMING *The act of inserting seeds into the soil with minimal soil disturbance. It is usually performed into the dead residue of the previous crop so that at least sixty percent of the ground is covered, which prevents soil erosion and retains soil moisture.*

In a letter to Charles W. Peale in 1813, Jefferson wrote, "We now plough horizontally following the curvatures of the hills and hollow, on the dead level, however crooked the lines may be. Every furrow thus acts as a reservoir to receive and retain the waters, all of which go to the benefit of the growing plant, instead of running off into streams."

No-till farming is a great conservation practice, but it is not the panacea of soil conservation. It takes a combination of conservation practices to anchor the soil and nutrients on the land where they belong, and keep them from washing away with rainfall into the streams, where they become pollutants.

Runoff from agricultural fields is one of the largest contributors of pollution to the streams in the Chesapeake Bay watershed. Planting annual crops such as corn, soybeans, and wheat has always had inherent risks for soil erosion and polluted runoff because these crops have to be planted every year. The steeper the land, the more conservation measures farmers need to apply to it to reduce erosion and increase the infiltration of water into the soil. Contour farming achieves both.

Biosecurity and Stream Exclusion

This is an adaptation of a "success story" written for the Chesapeake Bay Foundation that was published in May 2016.

Beef cattle biosecurity and stream exclusion are very important to Dr. Scott Nordstrom, a large animal veterinarian. On his first week on the job as a veterinarian in 1993, Nordstrom treated a case that would stick with him the rest of his life. Shockingly, half a herd of cattle he examined had died. It turned out that they had been stricken by bovine viral disease, BVD for short, a fatal condition transmitted from the intestines of one animal to the mouth of another.

Nordstrom set about finding out how the cattle got the disease. The next week, he was called to a farm just upstream with another case of BVD. He traced the source of the outbreak to that operation. "The stream carried the pathogens downstream, spreading it from one farm to the next," according to Nordstrom.

Since then, he's found time and again that as long as cattle are allowed in waterways, they risk catching diseases from farms upstream. "The biosecurity program for your cattle herd is no better than the worst farm upstream," says Nordstrom, now director of cattle technical services for an animal health company.

"If there is a disease outbreak in the herd upstream or even if they are just carriers of infectious organisms and they defecate in the stream, your animals are at risk if they drink from that stream," he explained.

Nordstrom travels all over the country to test vaccines for his animal health company. "In the large operations I have been on, they would never, ever, consider having their animals exposed to a stream or any other body of water," he says. "It's just too risky—for both livestock and people."

"Clearly, at least fifty percent of all cattle diseases in the Chesapeake Bay watershed are transmitted through the fecal-oral pathway," stresses Nordstrom. "Several of the big diseases in cattle are carried by water. These include BVD, leptospirosis, mastitis, cryptosporidiosis, and scours," he added.

BVD is spread by direct contact with the manure, urine, blood, mucus, and semen of infected animals. It causes diarrhea, nasal and ocular discharge, fever, lethargy, abortion, and sometimes death.

Leptospirosis, called lepto for short, is a bacterial disease that causes high fever, anemia, and death in three to five days in calves. For pregnant cows, it can cause embryonic death, abortions, retained placentas. It is a zoonotic disease, which means it can be transmitted to humans. It is often transmitted by direct contact with infected urine, placenta, or milk.

Mastitis is the inflammation of the mammary gland; it's most often caused by an infection. It is transmitted when cows drag their udders through pathogen-laden water or by flies or suckling calves.

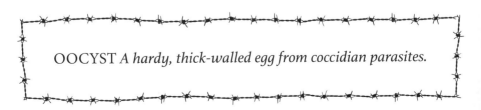

OOCYST *A hardy, thick-walled egg from coccidian parasites.*

Cryptosporidiosis, called crypto for short, is a disease caused by a protozoan that infects the intestinal lining of susceptible hosts. An infected animal can eject millions of oocysts in one bowel movement. Newborn and young calves ingesting these oocysts will become infected and get severe diarrhea.

Without treatment, they will die.

Scours is a term for diarrhea caused when the intestines become inflamed and cannot absorb liquids. Many pathogens can cause scours, including *E. coli*, salmonella, viruses, protozoans, and even yeasts and molds.

Vaccinating animals is a first line of defense against many diseases, but Nordstrom stresses that "the second line of defense is to fence livestock out of potentially infected waters."

Many programs are available that include funding and technical assistance to help farmers and land owners fence waterways and provide alternative sources of water for drinking. Nordstrom participated in the Conservation Reserve Enhancement Program (CREP) on his own farm. CREP is a joint federal, state cooperative program that helped design and fund stream fencing and livestock watering facilities. "We did it for herd health reasons; and besides, I feel good that the water leaving our farm is not going to infect animals downstream," he says.

Improve Herd Health with Abundant Clean Water

Humans don't drink dirty water and neither should your livestock. Aristotle recognized the value of boiling water and burying feces to prevent disease back in 350 BCE. We've been learning ever since. Just as with human health, herd health improves with abundant clean water.

Our veterinarian here at Meadowview is Dr. John Wise. "Abundant clean water is essential for the health of cattle," he says. "Lepto, *E. coli*, and mastitis are the main health problems with cattle drinking dirty water."

Even though there may not be much "peer-reviewed" published research documenting that drinking clean water improves herd health, I believe it is so. I have seen it with my own eyes, and many cattlemen have confirmed it through their observations. Our observations are referred to as "anecdotal" evidence, which means they are not based on scientific research.

As a farmer I don't need a research project to inform me that clean water is better for livestock than dirty water. I married a ninth-generation farmer: Jeanne Trimble Hoffman, a.k.a. the Princess of Swoope. She has a lot of experience with cattle. I call her a cow whisperer. Here's how she describes her experience with clean water and cattle: "All four of our herds receive the same vaccinations (same time, same drugs), and yet the herd that drinks out of a stream consistently does not do as well. The only difference in these groups is their water source."

We calve in the spring. In addition to the mature cows, we usually have between fifteen and twenty-five heifers that we keep near the house so we can watch them closely and assist them if needed. When a heifer calves, we make sure the baby has nursed and can follow its mother. We then move the mother and her baby to an adjacent field. The only water in that field used to be a couple of wet-weather streams and a pond.

For years, every year, these calves would come down with scours soon after we put them in the field with the pond. Scours is a condition in young calves that gives them diarrhea, which causes dehydration and sometimes death. Some say calf scours causes more financial loss in the cow-calf business than any other illness.

We knew the cause could not be the lack of colostrum because the mothers and calves were healthy going into the field. The cause was the pathogen-laden water that they were drinking.

Eventually, we convinced the owner of the field to allow us to fence the cows out of the wet areas and install a frost-free trough on high ground with good water. We have not had a case of scours in the field since we completed that project.

My good friend Gerald Garber, part owner of a large dairy farm in Weyers Cave, Virginia, weighed in on the subject. "There's no advantage to having cows in a stream," he opined. "It's bad for their health, and it pollutes the water."

Cattle do bad things in streams. They pollute the water, destroy aquatic ecosystems, and tear up the streambanks. Excluding livestock from streams is a high priority for all the states in the Chesapeake Bay watershed. Livestock exclusion and riparian forest buffers are two important best management practices in the Chesapeake Clean Water Blueprint.

There are many reasons to keep livestock out of streams and other wet areas. Herd health is one. Another is eliminating calving risk areas. Just about every livestock farmer I know has had a calf perish in a stream or wet area. Here's a typical scenario: a cow has some discomfort in labor, she goes to water, has her baby, and the baby cannot stand up because it's steep and rocky or because he gets sucked into the swamp. The calf dies of exposure.

Lose a calf today, you lose over one thousand dollars. A fence to keep calves out of risk areas is good insurance against this type of loss.

 ## It's Time to Get Down to Earth on Fighting Phosphorus Pollution—Use a Soil Test

This is an op-ed piece distributed by the Bay Journal News Service on February 3, 2015.

Maryland's newly elected governor, Larry Hogan, recently repealed the state Department of Agriculture's Phosphorus Management Tool (PMT) regulation. His act made me gnash my teeth.

Farmers and legislators on the Eastern Shore had begged him to repeal the regulation because it would have forced many of them to cease applying phosphorus-laden poultry litter to soils already saturated with the nutrient. Those farmers would instead be forced to use commercial fertilizer with no phosphorus to balance nutrient application with crop needs.

> PHOSPHORUS *An essential nutrient for plant growth. Plants use it for cell division and growth, and farmers apply it to crop fields through commercial fertilizer or manure. In excess, this nutrient becomes a pollutant in streams, rivers, and estuaries. This pollution usually occurs in areas that have more livestock, such as dairy and poultry operations, than there is land to safely apply the manure generated from these operations.*

Decades of repeated animal manure applications have overloaded many fields with phosphorus in the Bay watershed, including the Eastern Shore. Many of these soils have so much phosphorus that it leaches through the soil to the groundwater which enters surrounding streams and the Chesapeake Bay.

In the Chesapeake Bay watershed, seventy-five to one hundred percent of the soil tests conducted on farm fields on the Eastern Shore of Maryland and Virginia, parts of the Shenandoah Valley, and the Lancaster County region of Pennsylvania, have "excessive or optimum levels" of phosphorus.

Crops planted on these fields will not respond to additional inputs of phosphorus. Additional applications of phosphorus on these fields will leach into the groundwater or run off and become a water pollutant causing algae blooms, dead zones, and weakened aquatic ecosystems. Society as whole is paying hundreds of millions of dollars for nutrient management practices on farms to correct these abuses, but we are making very little progress.

Our tax dollars pay for nutrient management plans and planners, the development of "phosphorus indexes," the PMT, cover crops, and all sorts of fancy combinations of crop management techniques that look good on paper but do little to reduce excess nutrients in the water. The results are inflated or misleading numbers.

Survey after survey shows that people don't mind subsidizing farmers when they are doing things that improve natural resources. Personally, I loathe subsidizing farmers who continue to pollute even though the light of science is blazing in everyone's eyes—including theirs.

This scenario has been going on for decades all over the country where poor land-use practices pollute water and affect everything downstream. Science finds a solution—polluters whine and bellyache while politicians delay action. Science then finds another solution but makes things even more complicated—polluters continue to whine and bellyache while politicians delay action. It's the endless do-nothing loop. The result is more bureaucracy and paperwork as well as inflated, valueless data that make us feel as if progress is happening while in reality, only a tiny incremental change occurs.

The housing bubble that created our most recent economic recession was caused by inflated values, lack of regulatory oversight, and politicians not paying attention to sound management. These same toxic principals—inflated values, lack of oversight, and, in the case of the PMT, a disregard for science—are causing a nutrient-reduction bubble in the Chesapeake Bay watershed and beyond. In other words, we think we are reducing nutrients in the Bay but we really aren't.

The answer to this nutrient management problem is very simple and could save us millions of dollars.

Use a soil test.

If the nutrients are already in the soil to feed the crop, don't apply more. Use the money from all the crazy, complicated formulas that document the false reductions to move the nutrients to fields that could use them or transform them into something useful.

Phosphorus is a valuable nutrient that is needed worldwide. It is in short supply globally and, unlike nitrogen, cannot be manufactured. Conserving it and moving it to deficient areas makes sense. Manure transport and transformation programs need to be improved, verified, and fully funded.

In the poultry industry, nearly all the birds raised in this country are owned by very large corporations. These big poultry companies, called integrators, bring the phosphorus in through feed they purchase from the Midwest. The farmer, who works under contract to the integrators, feeds it to the chickens. But right now, it's the farmer, who most likely took out a loan to build those poultry houses, who is left with the debt, any dead birds, and the manure. It's an out-of-balance scenario all the way around.

Everyone involved is partly to blame, but they can all be part of the solution. Farmers need to fertilize according to a soil test; integrators need to take more ownership of the manure; scientists and environmentalists need to make solutions simpler; and politicians need to act based on science. I promise, if everyone does his part, society as whole will be willing to pay for it.

How We Live with the River on Our Cattle Farm

This week's flood prompted this essay on how we deal with floodwater from our river and a cattle operation. It was an out-of-bank flood event, but it didn't wash out our cattle crossing because we've learned to work with the river, not against it.

Our river, the Middle River, bubbles up out of the ground six miles upstream. By the time it reaches our farm it's about nine feet wide. It flows for a half mile through our pastures.

Middle River is a tributary of the South Fork of the Shenandoah River. It's the largest and longest river in the county, and it's on the state's Impaired Waters List for fecal coliform from cattle and lack of a benthic community, in other words, few water creatures live in the river. Macroinvertebrates, such as insects and other animals, make up the benthic community that helps define a clean stream. Sediment in water is lethal to a benthic community. Cattle going up and down the stream banks dislodge soils, which enter the steam and clog macroinvertebrate gills.

In order for Middle River to be delisted as an impaired stream and be restored, we have to fence cattle out of it. Cattle pollute the river with their feces and urine and trample the stream banks with their hooves. Their feces contain the fecal coliform that put the river on the list. We know this from antibiotic resistance analysis (ARA) testing. In addition, cow manure adds nitrogen, phosphorous, and pathogens that not only pollute the water but can compromise biosecurity for downstream livestock and humans.

The problem with fencing cattle out of the river is that the river floods, which can severely damage fences or take them out altogether. We learned a long time ago that you couldn't fight the river; it's going to flood, so you must work with it—not fight it. The secret to long-lived riparian fences is to build them outside the floodplain or put up inexpensive fences that effectively keep cattle out of the river and can be easily replaced when flood water damages them.

We installed a single strand of barbed wire in the floodplain, parallel to the river, and charged it with solar power. We get between 3,500 and 6,800 volts on the wire. A single hot (electrified) barbed-wire fence works with our cattle. We could have used smooth electrified wire, but for our cattle, it's not as effective at keeping them out of the river. Sometimes floodwaters go over the top of the fence and the barbs collect debris. It's easy to walk along and just lift or shake the debris off. We have not lost a single post or any line fences by using this method.

We did not want to use a more substantial fence because floodwaters would take it out, and we'd have to spend a lot of money and time to replace it.

At our river crossing, we put up a two-stage water gap using a single strand of electric polytape on each side of the sixteen-foot-wide crossing. When the river level is at normal flow or below, we use the lower stage, so cattle can cross and drink water from this access point. When the river is going to flood or when we don't have any cattle in that field, we move the polytape to a higher position on the fence posts so floodwater can pass under it. We have also rigged this crossing to break away should floodwaters bring enough force to rip it out.

Fencing cattle out of any stream will improve its water quality. Once the cows are out, a benthic community can thrive. All that manure that went downstream will instead be fertilizer for the pasture. Stream fencing has other benefits as well, such as creating more stable stream banks that don't crumble into the water and making more wildlife habitat. Cleaner streams in the headwaters of our Middle River help everyone downstream and will help restore the Chesapeake Bay.

Chesapeake Lessons for the Great Lakes

Sandusky, Ohio. It was dark as I drove into the roller coaster capital of the world—Cedar Point amusement park, on the shores of Lake Erie. There were life-size mummies, monsters, goblins, and witches all over the place. There was one Frankenstein-looking monster with Donald Trump hair. "Oh, I get it. They decorated for Halloween," I thought. I had to laugh. Here I was, entering a conference about water quality in the Great Lakes surrounded by roller coasters and haunted creatures.

One of my long-time mentors, Verna Harrison, asked me to help her present a program to a group of people in the Great Lakes region on the benefits of having a regional plan for clean water

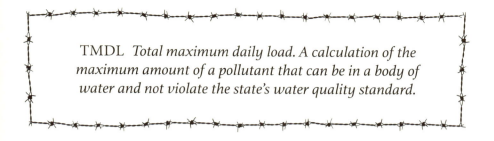

TMDL *Total maximum daily load. A calculation of the maximum amount of a pollutant that can be in a body of water and not violate the state's water quality standard.*

like we have in the Chesapeake Bay watershed. It was the twelfth annual conference of the Great Lakes Coalition.

This place, the Great Lakes, has certainly had its roller coaster rides and haunts regarding its water too. Talk about scary things: Toledo, on the southwestern shore of Lake Erie, had a toxic algae bloom in 2014 that shut down the city's water supply for three days, and Flint, Michigan, still has lead poisoning from its drinking water infrastructure.

The Chesapeake Bay, on the other hand, has had a steady, albeit slow, journey toward being restored. We have a regional plan to restore the Bay and the streams that feed it. It's called the Chesapeake Clean Water Blueprint or the Chesapeake TMDL. According to the EPA, the Blue Crab population is up ninety-two percent from last year (2015), water clarity is the best it has been in fifteen years, dead zones are shrinking, and all the Bay states except Pennsylvania are on track to meet their 2017 TMDL nutrient and sediment reduction targets.

The panel also included Cassandra Pallai, geospatial project manager with the Chesapeake Conservancy; Verna Harrison, principal, Verna Harrison Associates LLC; and Jeff Corbin, former EPA senior advisor to the administrator for the Chesapeake. We were there to discuss "Lessons from the Chesapeake."

From an agricultural standpoint, what could I share with the group assembled in Sandusky? I thought long and hard and came up with four lessons: (1) Why our plan, the Chesapeake Clean Water Blueprint, is working; (2) How to make nutrient management simpler; (3) How to monitor and verify cover crops via remote sensing; and (4) The need to invest in buffers and buffer maintenance.

The Chesapeake Clean Water Blueprint

Our number one lesson for the group was that the Chesapeake Clean Water Blueprint is working. Our Bay is improving. We have reduced nutrients in the Bay by half since 1983, despite a population increase of thirty percent. That is quite an achievement.

There are many reasons for this success: improvements in processing waste water, implementation of best management practices on farmland, successful oyster restoration, air pollution reduction, reductions in phosphorus from laundry detergent and lawn fertilizers, people doing their part, and I could go on and on.

The river that flows through our farm is a TMDL stream. This designation has brought program funds into our watershed to help farmers install needed best management practices like planting cover crops, crop rotation to perennials, and the establishment of riparian buffers. Because of these programs, our farm now produces food and clean water, something of which we are very proud. These programs created jobs for fence builders, excavation companies, tree planters, and other contractors

Those of us in the environmental community think our progress is woefully slow, but in truth, we are and have been improving the streams and waterways of the Bay slowly but steadily since we started the journey in the late sixties.

Make Nutrient Management Simpler

Chesapeake Bay farmers have greatly improved the use of nutrients on their land, and we have developed programs to transport poultry litter from areas with too much of it to areas that need it as fertilizer. But when it comes to phosphorous (P), programs have gotten too complicated and we have not done enough.

The government has built billion-dollar nutrient management bureaucracies, created phosphorous indexes, and developed management tools that hardly anyone understands. Nutrient management plans have been developed for farmers that often sit on a shelf. Many research dollars have been spent figuring out how we can keep applying phosphorus to soils already saturated with it, which is a waste of time and money avoiding the inevitable: if the soil is saturated with P, don't apply anymore. Period, with a capital P.

We should invest program dollars in bigger and better P (manure) transport to areas that need it. Phosphorus is a macronutrient in great demand. There are more acres of farmland that need P than acres that have too much.

We also need to begin using crops to remove P from soils saturated with it. Many say this form of P extraction from the soil, using crops, would take thirty to one hundred years. Okay, when do we start? Or do we just keep adding phosphorus?

Use Cover Crops but Make Verification Simpler

Farmers in the Chesapeake Bay watershed are planting cover crops like nowhere else. In most areas in Virginia for example, cover crop acres protect ninety percent of land planted to annual crops This is wonderful and reduces both soil erosion and nutrient runoff. Sadly, I was told that the best cover crop county in the Great Lakes region is at best five percent.

Virginia's cover crop program is a huge success, but it wastes money in verification and we've made to too complicated. To verify that a farmer has planted a cover crop in Virginia's cost share program, government employees drive around in their government vehicles to verify when the crop was planted and if and when the crop was harvested or killed. The programs even dictate what seeds the farmer can use as a cover crop. Most of this "on the ground" verification could be done remotely and that would save a lot of time and money.

To streamline the process, just let farmers know that their row-crop acres need to be one hundred percent covered by December 1. Farmers, I guarantee, will figure out how to get there. We don't need to dictate what seeds they use or when they must plant.

Riparian Forest Buffers Work but Need Maintenance

Streams flowing through a forest buffer are two to eight times more capable of reducing in-stream pollutants than streams flowing through grassed buffers. That's because leaves from native trees feed the bugs that eat the pollution. This empirical data comes to us from the Stroud Water Research Center.

Investing in trees along streams makes sense, and Chesapeake Bay farmers have planted thousands of acres of riparian forest buffers. To ensure success and improve the marketability of these nutrient-filtering carbon sinks, we need to invest more in maintaining these areas. We can't just plant the trees and walk away expecting a healthy forest in ten years.

The Chesapeake Clean Water Blueprint is working. The Bay is getting better and so are the streams that feed it. People from the Great Lakes are in great need of improved nutrient management, cover crops, and forest buffers. They can look to the Chesapeake Bay watershed for a path forward.

10

Bird Species in Steep Decline in Europe

Northern Bobwhite

"Just because the problem seems unsolvable doesn't give us the right to give up."

I can't remember who wrote that but it sticks in my mind. And just like the people trying to find that one blight-resistant American Chestnut tree, Northern Bobwhite lovers keep hoping that maybe someday one mating pair from pen-raised birds will survive and reproduce. We haven't found the resistant chestnut tree nor have we had success with reestablishing bobwhites using pen-raised birds . . . but it doesn't stop us from trying.

The Northern Bobwhite, also called bobwhite or simply quail, is the only partridge found in Virginia. It is a ground-dwelling bird about the size of a softball.

October 24 2013

5:15 a.m. Thirty-four degrees. The air is thick with moisture and the moon lights my way down the path to the river. I carry a small cage with ten pen-raised Northern Bobwhites. The Indian Grass, Big Bluestem, and other native grasses arch over my head. The mowed path crunches under my feet. Now on the bank of the river, I set the carrier down and then scatter some mixed birdseed around. The moon's reflection is on the river. With a silent reverence for nature and faith in the process of life, I open the door to the crate. "Good luck, my friends. May you have good health and prosper," I tell them. I turn and walk away; the soft wind ruffles the seed heads of the native grasses. The riffles of the river fade.

The odds of survival for these birds is pretty close to zero, but if just one pair survives the gantlet of hawks, falcons, foxes, domestic cats, and other predators through the winter, then just maybe they will reproduce. The ones we set out last year didn't make it.

Thanks to our friends in Middlebrook and Swoope who agreed to be part of the restoration effort, we released sixty-six birds last night on five separate farms with good quail habitat.

Quail populations began plummeting in the Shenandoah Valley of Virginia in the late seventies. Today the Northern Bobwhite is one of the Audubon Society's "common birds" in decline. Its population declined eighty percent since 1967. Why? We really don't know, but we have lots of theories. Many people and organizations, like the National Bobwhite Conservation Initiative, are trying to find out.

My opinion? Death by a thousand cuts.

Over ninety million domestic cats roam free. They are invasive and nonnative.

Tall Fescue, with its poisonous endophyte, dominates our grasslands; it is also invasive and nonnative.

Hedgerows and weedy odd areas that bobwhites need for habitat continue to diminish.

Mowed and manicured is the "look" everyone wants but provides zero habitat.

No one traps anymore, so we have more egg predators like raccoons, skunks, and opossums.

No bounties are placed on hawks anymore, so we have more raptors preying on quail.

I'm not blaming the natural predators; quail have always rebounded from natural dangers. In my opinion, the three biggest threats to quail are the unnatural ones—domestic cats, Tall Fescue, and lack of habitat.

Habitat restoration is the best hope for bobwhites. Here's what you can do: Plant native prairie meadows and shrub thickets. Suppress natural succession with fire and disturbance. Leave some areas unmowed. Plant food plots or leave some grain in the field.

Also, keep cats indoors! Domestic cats are the most destructive nonnative mammal in North America.

Loggerhead Shrike

Over the years they slowly disappeared. And then they were gone. I last saw a Loggerhead Shrike in Swoope in 2014. According to the National Audubon Society the Loggerhead Shrike is a "common bird" whose population is in "steep decline."

The Loggerhead Shrike is a songbird with a raptor beak. Often confused with the Mockingbird, the shrike has an unmistakable black mask and does not have the behavior or the song of the Mockingbird. Shrikes are carnivorous and stun their prey with their beak. The "Butcher Bird," as the shrike is known, impales its prey—such as small birds, small mammals, reptiles, and large insects—on thorns and barbed wire. Shrikes are rather hard to detect, and their song is not really a song at all but more of a shriek.

We used to see shrikes regularly. A nesting pair lived in the thorn bushes of an old hedgerow in the pasture behind the house. I lament that we may have had the last nesting pair in Augusta County on the farm where I live and work.

In the *News Leader* on March 3, 2006, the late Yulee Larner, Bird Lady of Augusta County, wrote the following about birding in Swoope: "This is the only place in Augusta County where we find nesting Bobolinks and the most consistent location for year-round records of the endangered Loggerhead Shrike."

I used to see shrikes every year somewhere in Augusta County, Virginia, in the eighties. We saw them in the backyard when we lived on Old Greenville Road in Mint Spring. I remember showing them to my daughter when she was young. She stood on a chair behind the sliding glass doors of the living room and observed them with my binoculars.

It was a rare bird even then, and to be honest, not many people even know about shrikes. They are about the same size and color as a Mockingbird. I'm a birder. And even in birding circles if you claim to have seen a Loggerhead Shrike, people tilt their head and squint one eye saying, "Oh, you probably just saw a Mockingbird."

Mockingbirds are not hard to find at all. They like to sit on a high perch, such as the top of a pole or on the top branch of a tall tree, and sing their hearts out with an infinite number of clear and vibrant songs. They often sing all day and into the night.

The Loggerhead Shrike is listed as "endangered" in Canada and either "threatened" or "endangered" in fourteen states including four states in the Chesapeake Bay watershed: Virginia, Maryland, Pennsylvania, and New York.

It is the only shrike species endemic to North America. Its population declined seventy-six percent between 1966 and 2015 according to the North American Breeding Bird Survey. Its population is expected to be cut in half again within twenty-four years, according to scientists at Partners in Flight. Globally, it's a "common bird" because its population is stable in the southern parts of its range in Texas, Florida, and Georgia. But in its transitional or migratory range, which includes Virginia, it is on the brink of extirpation.

"There are only about a hundred individual Loggerhead Shrikes left in Virginia and only a few known breeding pairs," laments Dr. Amy Johnson, director of Virginia Working Landscapes, a program of the Smithsonian Conservation Biology Institute.

No one can really pinpoint why the bird's population in the migratory zone has declined so rapidly. Scientists speculate that chemical pesticide use, loss of habitat, and climate change are partly to blame.

According to the Cornell Lab of Ornithology: "Loggerhead Shrikes have been listed as endangered, threatened, or of special concern in several states and Canada, and have been proposed for federal listing (the subspecies that nests on San Clemente Island, California, is listed as endangered). The species' decline coincides with the introduction and increased use of chemical pesticides between the 1940s and the 1970s, and may result in part from the birds' ingestion of pesticide-laced prey from treated fields."

Biologists from the Virginia Smithsonian Conservation Biology Institute have partnered with Wildlife Preservation Canada and the Toronto Zoo to support an ongoing reintroduction program. Using birds acquired from the Toronto Zoo, they are breeding Loggerhead Shrikes at the Smithsonian Zoo's facilities in Front Royal, Virginia, and transporting captive-bred juveniles into Canada to be released each year with juveniles from the Ontario program. Their hope is that this will enhance efforts to repopulate this migratory subspecies to its former range while enabling biologists to learn valuable information about their reproductive biology.

The Virginia Department of Game and Inland Fisheries and the West Virginia Department of Natural Resources are also involved with the reintroduction program.

The plan is working!

In 2017, one bird, raised in captivity and banded in Canada was seen in Augusta County, Virginia. It was captured on video by citizen scientist Jean Shutt.

You can help bring back the Loggerhead Shrike by maintaining critical habitat, contributing to wildlife habitat organizations, observing and reporting sightings, and by keeping cats indoors.

Shrikes prefer shrubby, thorny habitat for nesting and open pasture for hunting. Red Cedar, Osage Orange, and Hawthorns are their preferred nesting trees, according to Dr. Johnson. Hedgerows with these trees adjacent to grazed pasture are ideal but lone trees and shrubs in pastures are beneficial as well. Contact your local USDA office or your state's wildlife conservation office for assistance in establishing habitat.

Many organizations are working to establish and maintain wildlife habitat for Loggerhead Shrikes and other birds with populations in decline. Join them, volunteer for them, and contribute money to their cause.

If you see a Loggerhead Shrike, be very observant. Identify the bands on the legs (if present) and watch its behavior. Write down the location and time of day and report your sighting to your state's wildlife conservation office.

The domestic cat is the number one killer of birds in America. Keep your cat indoors and promote programs that foster the humane reduction of feral cat populations.

Horned Lark

As we drove into the pasture with a half-ton bale of hay for the cows, I saw a flock of perhaps thirty small birds fly in a tight pattern away from us.

The flying flock turned one way, then another, their white bellies exposed as they turned. This is a telltale sign of Horned Larks. They landed on the cold, brown, dormant pasture about thirty yards away. Once they landed, I could not see them with my naked eye because they blend in so well with the vegetation.

I don't think most people know what the birds are because they can't get close enough to identify them. They're just little birds flitting away. But train a pair of binoculars on them, and you will see one of the most beautiful birds in North America.

Horned Larks are the only true lark on the continent. Larks are characterized by a long hind claw. They have small tufts of feathers on their head that makes them look like they have horns.

Horned Larks are grassland birds, seven to eight inches long, brownish on top and white underneath. They have a white eye-stripe, black mustache, yellow chin, and black bib. They prefer very short vegetation or bare ground, and they walk or run along the ground in search of seeds and insects.

The vast grasslands of Swoope, Virginia, are in America's legendary Shenandoah Valley. We see Horned Larks every day during the winter in fields where we feed the cows. In these fields, the vegetation is short but not bare. I don't see them in the summer on the farm because the grasses are too high for them.

Sadly, this bird is also a common bird in steep decline. "Horned Lark populations have plummeted more than seventy percent since 1970," according to Partners in Flight. The reasons for the decline are all anthropogenic (human-induced) and include loss of habitat, urbanization, and pesticides

"Horned lark populations have steadily declined as dry, open uplands have reverted to forests or have been destroyed by development. As with other ground-nesting birds, high populations of predators, such as raccoons, skunks, and housecats, have also contributed to the decline of this species," states a report from the Connecticut Department of Energy and Environmental Protection that lists the bird as "state endangered."

On the bright side, scientists report that the Horned Lark is a "super avoider" of collisions with towers and buildings.

Larks are year-round residents in most of the continental U.S. Their breeding range extends into Canada and above the Arctic Circle.

How can you help?

There are several ways. Support Farm Bill legislation that conserves grassland. Support local ordinances that prevent the conversion of agricultural land to nonagricultural uses. Keep cats indoors, and support programs that humanely trap, neuter, and shelter feral cats.

Yellow-Billed Cuckoo

I once watched a Yellow-Billed Cuckoo devour a whole nest of destructive Eastern Tent Caterpillars. Yellow-Billed Cuckoos—we need a lot more of them. The Yellow-Billed Cuckoo, sometimes called the rain crow, nests and forages in the riparian forests along our part of the Middle River. Not many birds eat hairy caterpillars, but Yellow-Billed Cuckoos prefer them.

The Eastern Tent Caterpillar, native to North America, prefers to lay eggs and build silken nests in native Black Cherry trees. During the heat of the day, the caterpillars hide and rest in their silken nest. At night or early morning when it is cool, they come out and consume the host tree's leaves, often defoliating the entire tree, but cuckoos sweep in during the day, rip the nest open, and devour the resting caterpillars.

Yellow-Billed Cuckoos are about the size of a Blue Jay but with a long, banded tail. They are difficult to see because they remain so still for long periods. They have a distinct call, however, that is unmistakable—kuk, kuk, kuk, kuk, keow.

These beautiful birds were not on this farm fifteen years ago because there weren't enough trees along the river to attract them. In 2004, we fenced the cows out of the river and planted native trees along the banks, creating a riparian forest. Today many of our trees are over fifteen feet tall and are host to not only the Yellow-Billed Cuckoo but many other riparian forest birds such as the Willow Flycatcher, Yellow Warbler, Warbling Vireo, and both Baltimore and Orchard Orioles.

Nonbreeding Yellow-Billed Cuckoos do not migrate. Breeding birds, however, migrate from South America to North America to breed and raise their young. Migrating birds travel north through Mexico and when they arrive at the Southern tip of the Rocky Mountains they split into two distinct population segments—the western segment and the eastern segment.

The Western Distinct Population Segment was listed as "threatened" under the Endangered Species Act by the U.S. Fish and Wildlife Service on October 3, 2014. The reason for the drastic population collapse in the West is the destruction of riparian forests for agriculture and urban development. Scientists believe the western cuckoo populations have been extirpated or wiped out completely from British Columbia, Washington, Oregon, and Nevada.

Here in the East and in the Chesapeake Bay watershed, the population of Yellow-Billed Cuckoos is considered common but in steep decline, losing fifty-two percent of its numbers in the past forty years, according to Partners in Flight, a conservation organization with over 150 partner organizations throughout the Western Hemisphere.

A riparian forest provides many benefits. Increased wildlife diversity is only one. Improving water quality in a stream is another. Native trees along a stream provide leaves for the aquatic bugs to eat. Leaves are the corn silage of the aquatic ecosystem. A thriving, healthy aquatic ecosystem is two to eight times more capable of processing in-stream pollution than a nonforested riparian buffer, according to the Stroud Water Research Center.

Wildlife will come and our streams will become cleaner when we plant more riparian forests. It's one of the most important and cost-effective practices to restore the waters of not only the Chesapeake Bay but the waters of the world. We enrolled in USDA's Conservation Reserve Program in 2004, but many other programs can also assist with establishing streamside forests.

11
Invasive Species

Invasive Species Defined

The definition of an invasive species of the United States (ISOTUS) is "any organism not found naturally occurring in the ecosystem under consideration and causes or is likely to cause environmental or economic harm or causes or is likely to cause harm to human health."

There are so many invasive species...

It is extremely difficult for me to articulate, in prose, my feelings about how damaging and invasive humans are—the most profound example of damage being human-induced climate change. At first, I thought about how invasive certain plants are to local plant communities like thistles are to pasture. Then I lamented the loss of our vast native grasslands to Tall Fescue, possibly the most invasive nonnative plant in North America. Mankind's lust for profit is the most likely driving force behind the damage caused by invasive species.

Expanding this notion of humans causing the invasiveness of plants and animals to diseases and even into world politics and climate change led me to conclude that the whole subject is so complicated and so vast that I hardly understand it. Hence, the following poem.

Invasive We Are

Globalization and invasiveness began with the age of exploration,

    1492, Columbus, Catesby, Bartram, Jefferson,
    John Smith, English Sparrow, Starling, Honey Bee

    Transportation   Free Market

The intensity of invasiveness mirrors human growth,
Both now in the vertical stem of the Malthusian "J" Curve

    Kudzu, Ailanthus, Fescue, Brome
    Phragmites, Zebra Mussel, Emerald Ash Borer
    Gypsy Moth   Aids   Ebola   Zika

    American Chestnut, American Indian, Cerulean Warbler,
    Bobwhite Quail

Monoculture Biota,   Monoculture Politics,   Money

    Immigrant   Invasion   Invasive

    Explore   Exploit   Extinct

                                      Homogenized Earth

Why I Hate Tall Fescue

This op-ed was distributed by the Bay Journal News Service on May 27, 2014, and was titled "Please, Step on This Grass."

I was in the farm co-op store the other day in line to buy some garden seeds. The farmer in front of me ordered fifty pounds of Kentucky 31 Tall Fescue. I thought, "Oh my God, you poor dear, haven't you heard? Those seeds are infected with an internal fungus that secretes an alkaloid that will be toxic to your livestock."

We should not plant another seed of Tall Fescue. Not only is it invasive and nonnative (it's native to Europe), it is toxic to just about everything that consumes it, and it inhibits the growth of other plants.

Tall Fescue is one of the most dominant grasses found in pastures, hayland, lawns, roadsides, wetlands, and vacant lots throughout most of North America. It is almost always infected with an internal fungus, an endophyte, that produces an alkaloid, called ergovaline, that is toxic.

We've known for years about its grave effects on pregnant horses: abortions, thickened placentas, and limited milk. Cattle get "fescue toxicosis" or "summer slump," symptoms of which include elevated body temperature, hoof rot, tail rot, lower conception rates, and lower weight gain.

In wildlife biology fescue is known as the F-word. According to most wildlife biologists, it is the number one reason our Northern Bobwhite populations have plummeted. Tall Fescue forms a sod or mat so thick that a bird can't walk through it. Tall Fescue seeds are also toxic to birds. And fescue creates excellent habitat for meadow voles, which attract hawks, and hawks kill bobwhites.

Tall Fescue is toxic to just about anything that eats it. Google it. It's toxic to dairy cows, beef cows, horses, sheep, goats, birds, grasshoppers, ants, and even nematodes. It also cuts down on biodiversity because it takes up space that native biota could have occupied, and it's aggressive.

It's also toxic to newly planted tree seedlings. It's allelopathic, the name for what occurs when one plant exudes a substance into the soil that inhibits the growth of other plants. Allelopathic plants are one of the reasons many riparian forest buffer plantings fail. A two-year-old hardwood seedling inserted into a mature sod of Tall Fescue not only has to compete with the established fescue roots for nutrients and water, it has to overcome the toxins secreted by the endophyte in Tall Fescue.

Tall Fescue is persistent in the landscape. I call it the toxic waste of the grass kingdom. It is difficult to get rid of. I once had a client tell me he bought a farm with a pasture dominated by Tall Fescue. He wanted wildlife habitat. So he just "let it go," hoping natural succession would take place. Ten years later it looked exactly the same. The Tall Fescue formed such a dense mat that no seeds could get through it, and even if they did, the allelopathic toxins would have caused their demise.

So why does USDA still recommend it, and how did it get here in the first place? A brief history: Livestock farmers are always looking for grass that can produce feed for the longest period. University of Kentucky agronomists found what they thought was the holy grail of grasses in 1931 in a "holler" in the winter: it was green when all other grasses were dormant. They collected the plant and propagated it. The university released it in 1943 under the name Kentucky 31 Tall Fescue.

Oops. They did not know the plant had an internal fungus that produced an alkaloid that is toxic. We've been promoting it ever since, even though we discovered the toxic relationship in the 1970s.

Okay, I'll admit Tall Fescue is good for three things: erosion control, winter grazing, and wiping manure off your boots.

Tall Fescue is good for erosion control because it is aggressive and can withstand abuse. Cattlemen have been using it for years to "stockpile" for winter grazing. In other words, they take their cattle off it in August, fertilize it with nitrogen, let it grow, and then graze it during the winter. It is excellent forage in the winter because the toxins aren't active in cool temperatures.

It's everywhere and difficult to get rid of. So how do we deal with it? The first line of defense is to dilute it. Graze it hard and then overseed with clover. "Endophyte free" varieties of Tall Fescue exist, but they have not proven to be long lived.

Two effective ways to kill Tall Fescue include tilling it to death or a couple of applications of herbicide. Once the Tall Fescue has been killed, plant a more desirable forage.

The best remedy, though, is to never plant another seed of endophyte-infected Tall Fescue. Many other kinds of grass can produce forage for livestock without the side effects of the endophyte, such as Orchardgrass and Smooth Brome. Let's use them.

Four Compelling Reasons Cats Need to Be Kept Indoors

The debate between cat lovers and bird lovers is not a new one, and both sides are passionate. The debate usually ends in a stalemate, with the cat people having the last word: cats kill birds, but it's not the cat's fault; it's their nature. Rarely does the discussion deviate from these two fundamental issues. But the problems are much broader than just the fact that cats kill birds.

There are four compelling reasons to keep all cats indoors.

1. It's dangerous for cats to be outside.
2. Outdoor cats harm the environment.
3. Outdoor cats harm the economy.
4. Outdoor cats harm human health.

It's Dangerous for Cats to Be Outside

Indoor cats are great companion animals, giving pleasure to their owners. Outdoor cats—domestic and feral—are exposed to numerous threats such as cars, dogs, fleas, poison, rabies, owls, coyotes, foxes, and mean people. The Humane Society and PETA (People for the Ethical Treatment of Animals), as well as every wildlife conservation organization I am familiar with, recommends that *all* cats be indoor cats for their own good.

Outdoor Cats Harm the Environment

I have seen cats kill many birds. Years ago, when I lived in a small city, I built a bird sanctuary in our backyard. It had shrubs, flowers, and a pond with a waterfall. It attracted many birds—and my neighbor's cat. I saw that cat capture and kill a Golden-Winged Warbler, a very rare and beautiful bird. That experience was an epiphany. For the first time, I saw the cat as the nonnative killer it is. It made me gnash my teeth with anger. What right did my neighbor have to allow her cat to roam free into my space and kill birds?

Many scientific studies prove beyond a shadow of a doubt that cats, even when they are not hungry, kill birds, mammals, reptiles, and many other small animals. Cats are the number one killer of birds in the U.S., causing 1.3 to 4 billion deaths per year, according to scientists at the Smithsonian Migratory Bird Center. Domestic cats are responsible for the extinction of more than sixty species worldwide, including thirty-three species of birds such as the Chatham Rail. Outside, cats are the most destructive, nonnative mammal in North America.

Outdoor Cats Harm the Economy

Americans spent about 2.4 million dollars on animal welfare programs in 2007 according to one study by the Humane Society. Of course, that is not all for cats, but at least a significant portion of it is for cat shelters, euthanasia, and trap, neuter, and release programs.

Has your house ever been infested with fleas? Americans spend over nine billion dollars a year on flea control and flea eradication efforts. Outdoor cats are likely to bring fleas and their eggs into your house.

Up to sixty percent of all outdoor cats are infected with a protozoan that causes toxoplasmosis. If an infected barn cat defecates on the feed for sheep and goats, it is likely to infect a pregnant ewe or nanny. If it does, the nanny will likely abort her baby. Toxoplasmosis is one of the leading causes of abortion in the U.S. sheep industry.

American taxpayers spend millions of dollars on habitat establishment for threatened, endangered, and declining species such as the Northern Bobwhite and the Piping Plover. These two ground-nesting birds are heavily preyed on by mammalian predators. Outdoor cats are on the short list of culprits. We spend millions to protect birds yet allow cat lovers to shelter and feed feral cats that kill the birds on public land. The *Stevenson v. Galveston County* case and the *American Bird Conservancy v. Rose Harvey* case are classic examples of the bird lovers versus cat lovers debate still raging in America and throughout the world.

Jim Stevenson, founder of the Galveston Ornithological Society, killed a cat that was killing a Piping Plover, a federally listed threatened species under the U.S. Endangered Species Act. He was arrested and went to jail. Cat lovers called him a serial cat killer. Bird lovers hailed him as a torch bearer for protecting birds. The case resulted in a hung jury.

Rose Harvey is the commissioner of New York State Parks. He allowed cat lovers to regularly feed and erect shelters for feral cats in the Rose Hill State Park. The American Bird Conservancy sued him on the grounds that public servants violated the Endangered Species Act by not protecting Piping Plovers from being killed by feral cats. This case was settled on August 3, 2018 in federal court. All the cats must be removed, in as humane a manner as possible, from Jones Beach State Park by March 31, 2019.

Cats Harm Human Health

Many diseases can be transmitted from cats to humans. Elderly, pregnant, and immunosuppressed adults, as well as infants, are all susceptible to the following diseases: cat scratch fever, salmonella, scabies, internal parasites including roundworms and hookworms, ringworm, cryptosporidiosis, giardia, rabies, toxoplasmosis, and ailments caused by flea bites, including bubonic plague.

In 2017 cats were the fourth most common species testing positive for rabies by the Virginia Department of Health (raccoons were first, followed by skunks, and then foxes). Outdoor feeding stations for cats are magnets for wild animals such as raccoons and skunks that often transmit rabies to cats via their saliva or bites.

Toxoplasmosis, also known as "crazy cat lady syndrome," harms humans just as it harms livestock. Susceptible humans, like elderly people who have many cats, can ingest the *Toxoplasma gondii* protozoa from the litter box or contaminated soil. Symptoms include fatigue, fever, aches, pains lasting more than a month, seizures, confusion, and ocular ailments including redness of the eyes, reduced vision, pain, blurred vision, inflammation of the retina, and tearing.

It's not difficult for pet owners to keep their cats indoors. The bigger problem is the population of feral cats. There are between thirty-five and seventy-five million feral cats in America causing environmental, economic, and human health harm.

How does society deal with other feral animals such as pigs and pythons or goats on the Galapagos Islands? They eradicate them. Cats are different because they are companion animals.

But if feral cat populations aren't checked, they will continue to increase along with the problems associated with them. The answer is clear: gather the feral cats, neuter the feral cats, and place them in shelters and homes. Trap, neuter, and release programs do not work. The only answer is a trap, neuter, and shelter program.

As I have pointed out, the definition of invasive species of the United States is "any organism not found naturally occurring in the ecosystem under consideration and causes or is likely to cause environmental or economic harm or causes or is likely to cause harm to human health."

The domestic cat is not native to North America. It originated in the Middle East. The domestic cat meets every aspect of the definition of invasive species and is the most destructive nonnative mammal in North America.

House Sparrow

The House Sparrow is perhaps the most adaptable and prolific bird species on the planet. Often called English Sparrow, its scientific name, *Passer domesticus,* is Latin for "small, active bird belonging to the house." It is native to Europe and has spread to all corners of the world. Its adaptation follows human civilization. Where there are people, there are House Sparrows.

House Sparrows are cavity nesters. At six inches long, they are about the same size as Eastern Bluebirds and Tree Swallows. That's why they all compete for the same nest boxes. Make sure your boxes have an entry hole no larger than one inch in diameter. If the hole is larger, another invasive, nonnative European bird, the European Starling, will invade the box.

The House Sparrow is not native to North America. It is an aggressive species that will take over the nesting sites, territories, and food sources of native birds. Therefore, it is an invasive, nonnative species, and it is very difficult to manage.

House Sparrows Attack and Kill Nesting Native Birds

Some years ago, I opened one of our nest boxes to find a House Sparrow sitting on her eggs. She quickly flew away. Something was unusual. She had built her nest on top of a Tree Sparrow nest. I removed the aggressor's nest, tossed it on the ground and crushed the eggs. Underneath the nest was a dead female Tree Swallow. The aggressor had bashed in her head with its beak. How horrible a death. The Tree Swallow's eggs were still intact.

House Sparrow nests are easy to identify. House Sparrows always build a "dome" or roof over the nest, and the nest material is rather trashy, made up of all kinds of material including various feathers. The eggs are white with dark brown speckles.

If you find a dome-shaped, trashy nest with feathers in your nest box, take it out and destroy it. You will be helping native birds find a home. But be vigilant. The House Sparrow will be persistent, so you must be as well.

Native Plants Can Be Invasive

I finally found a plant that will take over Tall Fescue—Wingstem—but I'm not sure I like it. Let me explain.

Both plants are invasive. Tall Fescue is a nonnative, invasive plant; Wingstem is a native plant that is invasive.

What is an invasive plant? One definition is "any plant species whose introduction to the ecosystem under consideration will cause economic or environmental harm or harm to human health." Both native and nonnative plants can fit this definition.

Nonnative plants that cause economic or environmental harm include Kudzu, Canadian Thistle, Teasel, Tree of Heaven, Nut Grass, Johnsongrass, and Tall Fescue. The list is endless, and each item on it can cause economic and environmental damage.

But native plants can be invasive too. Goldenrod is a good example of a native plant that can be invasive. It can be a great plant in your garden—it has beautiful blooms and attracts many beneficial insects—but it can take over. To the nursery industry or to cattle farmers it can be a scourge, aggressively displacing more desirable plants. Goldenrod occupying the space where one wants native purple coneflower would have to be pulled up by hand, killed with herbicides, or controlled with some other method. It can take over a flowerbed or take over acres of pasture.

Another example of a potential native invasive is the Black Cherry Tree. Granted it is a grand tree with gorgeous wood and fruit for wildlife, but on a cattle farm, it is undesirable and invasive along hedgerows. Its wilted leaves are deadly to cattle.

In our riparian buffer along Middle River, we try to maintain an ecosystem that is as biodiverse as possible and includes trees, shrubs, forbs, and grasses—all native, of course. It isn't easy.

First, we fought Tall Fescue, and now we are fighting Wingstem—it's taking over! Wingstem is a delightful native plant, and we welcome some of it, but we don't want a monoculture of it. The cows would eat some of it, but we don't want our cows in the riparian area—they would also eat the trees we are nursing along. Our goal is biodiversity.

We are now mowing as much Wingstem as possible, but we will never get it all. When it resprouts, I will apply an herbicide to attempt to kill it. In late November, we will plant native shrubs and trees where the Wingstem was. It won't be the end of them. You can't plant your shrubs and trees and just walk away. Tending to a native community takes a lot of maintenance.

Emerald Ash Borer

The Emerald Ash Borer, is a destructive, nonnative insect that kills all species of ash trees. First discovered in the United States in Michigan in 2002, it has spread to thirty-three states and is confirmed in all six of the Chesapeake Bay watershed states. These insects have arrived in Augusta County, Virginia, in full force, infecting one of the most important riparian trees in the Chesapeake Bay watershed—Green Ash. To my chagrin, they are killing the ash trees on our farm.

This is bad news for riparian forest buffers. Green Ash is one our best trees because it populates on its own and is fast growing. Green Ash is one of the most important trees along streams and rivers. It is called a pioneer tree because it is one of the first trees to naturally populate areas along streams. Its seeds have evolved to be transported by wind and water.

At a time when many more acres of riparian forests are needed, we are losing a first-string player on our riparian forest buffer team. Luckily, we have a deep bench.

I first learned of Emerald Ash Borer destruction in Augusta County when Joe McCue, president of the Friends of Middle River and I were doing maintenance work on a riparian forest buffer along Middle River near Weyers Cave, Virginia. We walked along the rows of towering trees, pruning the lower limbs, removing tree shelters as needed and removing invasive species. The Green Ash trees didn't look too good.

The main stems of the Green Ash were dead on ninety percent of the trees. These dying trees had some new growth sprouting around the lower part of the trunk. This is called epicormic sprouting. It happens when the tree is on its last leg of life. The Emerald Ash Borer was responsible. The larval stage of the borer eats the vascular system of the tree, thereby cutting off the flow of nutrients and water to the rest of the tree.

Another telltale sign of Emerald Ash Borer infestation is the distinctive D-shaped exit hole in the bark when the adult leaves the tree.

There is not much we can do to prevent further infestation. For specimen trees, systemic insecticide treatments are available. Scientists have found several beneficial wasps that parasitize the borer and field trials have been successful.

One thing we can do is encourage and plant other native trees. Diversity in tree populations is very important because it makes the forest more stable to withstand stresses. Other pioneer species include American Sycamore, Box Elder, Red Maple, Black Locust, and Catalpa; encourage these trees by not mowing them down. Plant these and other trees such as Willow Oak, Swamp White Oak, Pawpaw, River Birch, and other trees suitable for the site and soil.

Quackgrass: Far Better Than Tall Fescue or Orchardgrass

Several days ago, we had "just one more" chore: letting the cows into the hay lot behind our neighbor's house so they could eat the grass down. There is no fence between the hay lot and hay field so we put up some fake electric fence (we didn't have any power to the wire but the cows didn't know that) and parked the truck outside it where we could sit and watch the cows eat.

I fixed us both an adult beverage—it was way past five o'clock, maybe six or seven. I sat on the back of the pickup truck while Jeanne called the cows. Within minutes the cows started filing into the small lot, and once the first couple of cows began eating the lush plants, the other cows quickened their pace.

The cellulose-digesting mobile protein and fertilizer factories that we call cows were munching down. I like to watch and listen to them eat, especially when I'm relaxing with an adult beverage.

I was curious as to what they would prefer to eat in this lot. It had many grass species: Orchardgrass, Tall Fescue, Cheat, Bluegrass, Smooth Brome, Tall Meadow Oat Grass, and another one I couldn't identify. Broadleaf plants included Wild Mustard, Musk Thistle, Virginia Pepperweed, and others.

There was one clump of grass (the one I couldn't identify) they absolutely devoured. They hit it once then hit it again and then came back and hit it again. It was the preferred plant—by far. They preferred it even over Orchardgrass. They even ate Wild Mustard before they ate the Orchardgrass or the Tall Fescue. Orchardgrass was just past the "boot stage" of maturity; that's when the seed heads are emerging from the sheath.

I picked some of the stems of the preferred plant and took them to the house, where I had a grass identification key I could use to find out what it was.

I was shocked to find that it was Quackgrass, another introduced species from Europe. It's the weed we hate in the garden because it spreads by rhizomes.

I did a little research and found that it's an amazing grass. In Europe, the roots are dried and fried; some say it tastes sweet and a little like licorice. It has medicinal values as well, such as curing kidney ailments. The roots can be dried and ground into a flour to make bread, and reportedly the roots can be boiled down to a syrup to make beer.

Here's a quote about Quackgrass from English botanist, herbalist, and physician Nicholas Culpepper in 1653: "Although a gardener be of another opinion, yet a physician holds half an acre of them to be worth five acres of carrots twice over."

This species of pasture grass has far more positive attributes than the invasive, nonnative, endophyte-infected, toxic Tall Fescue that USDA still recommends. Quackgrass is one species that could easily replace Tall Fescue for erosion control and forage.

EPILOGUE

Years ago, the communications director of the Chesapeake Bay Foundation asked me to write an article for Save the Bay *magazine. She asked me to write about what gives me hope. Below is the article from its winter 2014 edition.*

Harpers Ferry, West Virginia. There is a lot of history here—and a lot of water.

I can't drive through the town on U.S. Route 340 without stopping to walk across the pedestrian bridge spanning the Potomac River there. It's a religious kind of thing for me, walking across the nation's river, hearing and feeling the energy from the rolling water below.

I look downstream at the hole this great river carved through the Blue Ridge Mountains. It's an awesome sight. Thomas Jefferson wrote, "The passage of the Patowmac through the Blue Ridge is perhaps one of the most stupendous scenes in nature."

The river water below me came from rainwater that flowed across or through six million acres of land. The land and the soil within are the regulators of the entire hydrologic cycle. Land, with robust healthy soil, produces clean water. Just downstream to the right, the water from another two million acres joins the Potomac; it's the Shenandoah River. The farm I live on with my wife, Jeanne, our dog, Dexter, and a commercial herd of beef cattle is part of the beginning of that river, 135 miles upstream.

I have a picture of Harpers Ferry in my office in Swoope, Virginia. It was taken from a high bluff across the Potomac, and it shows the two rivers coming together. I like to show it to people and tell them that the water flowing across and through our farm empties into the South Fork of the Shenandoah River. I tell them, "The Chesapeake Bay begins here, in Swoope, Virginia." The restoration of the river and the Bay begins with what we do on our farm.

The Bay starts in tens of thousands of places just like ours throughout the sixty-four-thousand-square-mile watershed. Each person and each tributary makes a difference, and every person and every tributary will have to participate to achieve a restored Bay.

All the tributaries coming together to form the Potomac River overcame the physical barrier of the Blue Ridge Mountains. All of us, working together, can overcome the social barriers preventing a restored Bay—apathy and ignorance.

We are on an ambitious path to clean up our streams. It's called the Chesapeake Clean Water Blueprint. It's working. We've reduced nitrogen and phosphorus pollution by half since the 1980s—despite the thirty percent increase in the Bay watershed population.

In fact, according to the Chesapeake Bay Foundation's 2014 report, "The Economic Benefits of Cleaning Up the Chesapeake," a restored Bay will generate 130 billion dollars for our economy annually—22 billion dollars more per year than if we don't achieve a restored Bay. This is incredible.

Quite simply, there are no downsides to a restored Bay.

As I stand here on the bridge over the Potomac looking downstream, I see the sediment-laden waters of the Shenandoah joining the nation's river. When I see brown water, I lament that so much more needs to be done. People upstream didn't understand, or didn't care, that what they do on their land profoundly affects what's in the water and everyone downstream. We need to reach out to these people and help them understand that it's going to take every person and every tributary.

Standing on the pedestrian bridge over the Potomac, I feel the power of the river. It gives me hope that one day we will have a restored Middle River in Swoope and a restored Chesapeake Bay.

ABOUT THE AUTHOR

Robert "Bobby" Whitescarver is a watershed restoration scientist, farmer, award-winning writer, and educator. He retired from the USDA's Natural Resources Conservation Service with thirty-one years of field experience. He has helped farmers all over Virginia exclude livestock from more than six hundred miles of streambanks and plant over a half million hardwood trees. Bobby and his wife, Jeanne Trimble Hoffman, operate a commercial cow-calf operation in Swoope, Virginia.

Bobby is president of Whitescarver Natural Resources Management LLC, an environmental consulting firm. He also teaches Natural Resource Management at James Madison University and is a freelance writer. His award-winning blog can be found at www.gettingmoreontheground.com.

He has a bachelor's degree in agronomy from Virginia Tech and a master's degree in public administration from James Madison University.

In 2002, the Chesapeake Bay Foundation chose him as its Conservationist of the Year. He received James Madison University's Provost Award for Excellence in Teaching in 2018. Also in 2018, Bobby and Jeanne were chosen as Hugh Hammond Bennett Conservation Excellence Farmers by the National Conservation Planning Partnership. Bobby is recognized by the National Association of Conservation Districts as a Soil Health Champion.